THINGS
Common
and Preferred

Christian
Perspectives...

THINGS

Common

and

Preferred

Christian Perspectives...

by

KARL A. OLSSON

Augsburg Publishing House • Minneapolis, Minnesota

The Library of Congress has cataloged this book as follows:

Olsson, Karl A.
   Things common and preferred; Christian perspectives.
Minneapolis, Augsburg Pub. House [1959]

   181 p.   21 cm.

        1. Civilization, Christian.   I. Title.

BR115.C505   242   59-6680

Library of Congress

THINGS COMMON AND PREFERRED

Christian Perspectives . . .

Manufactured in the
United States of America

Foreword

In the spring of 1955 the editor of our denominational weekly extracted a promise from me to write a column for his paper. I had done this sort of thing years before, but the paper for which I wrote became a depression casualty, and now I wasn't sure that I had either the time or the inclination for this kind of writing. The inducement to do it was a blank check—I could write on anything or everything as long as it was done from a Christian perspective.

I have done literally that. To begin with, some readers demurred. They felt that I wasn't devotional enough, that I strayed too far from the path of "Christian writing." When I proclaimed that the world was my oyster, an unhappy reader asked that I prepare something other than oyster stew. But in the main the reaction was favorable. Most people realized that I was trying to come to them where they lived and that I was trying to say something about the good gray world in which all of us spend most of our time. What I have tried to say about this world is that it is Christ's world. He rules not only in the churches but in the supermarkets and the summer cottages; even when we are figuring the income tax, we are not alone.

If I am indebted to anyone for this perspective, I suppose it is C. S. Lewis, whose *Screwtape Letters* opened up a new universe when I first read it during the war. But I have not tried to copy anyone, and my perspectives are my own, for better or for worse.

Interest in the column has led to the publication of this collection in book form. I am indebted to the COVENANT WEEKLY, where these columns first appeared, and to its editor, Carl Philip Anderson, not only for permission to reprint but for encouragement and invaluable suggestions.

KARL A. OLSSON

Contents

Contents

I Wish They'd Stop Smiling

The Cult of
Reassurance

If you get your cultural history from novels—a most pain-less method—you have probably been aware of the way in which in times past occupations shaped character. If during the 19th century you were a physician, you were grave and bearded and had spatulated fingers with large, almond-shaped nails cut square. If you were a solicitor, you were probably yellowed like parchment with a paper-thin voice and a fussy way of handling the goose quill pen. If you were a clergyman, you were either the hearty, beef-eating type, all guff and gaw, who rode to hounds before breakfast, came booted under the surplice, knew Aristophanes better than the Apostles, and died of an apoplexy *or* you were long, thin, and desperate with Low Church convictions on most matters, a harridan of a wife in bombazine, and a half-completed treatise on Rufinus. And if you were an undertaker, you were just gloomy.

Now all that has changed. The sublime, the perilous, the sober, and the trivial vocations have all been bathed in

1

the same solution. Whether you are a clown or have only one facade when you meet the Public—you SMILE. Gone is the nobly-tilted head and the bestroked beard of the doctor, the mumbled Latinities, the sad verbiage: clysters, irrigations, compresses, salts, potions, pills, powders. Gone is the stiff brocade of legal jargon, the whereases, to-wits, sames and saids, behind which twitched the dry little monkey face of Fleet Street, all dignity and celluloid collars. Gone is the crude joviality, the unwashed heartiness of the worldly vicar, and the wax-yellow, vinegary primpishness of the unworldly one. Gone is the granite face of the sea. Gone almost is the bitterness of the coalstreaked toiler. Gone too the final dreariness of the Embalmer, the black gloves, the horse face elongated further by professional grief, the stilted sigh, the stilted smirk.

Cheer and Chiclets

Now if your plane is plummeting earthward and you are pulling yourself together for the last Adventure, a blonde girl with freshly-brushed teeth impales you on her smile and hands you a fruit drop. You take it with the desperate glance of a man being given his viaticum, but the smile never wavers. You are being reassured.

Or your whole lower jaw is a mass of pain and you know that this is going to involve a cabinet full of drills, augers, awls, pincers, elevators, pliers, chisels, lancets, and scalpels. There is the smell of iodoform in the air, banana oil and essence of cloves. There is the rustle of freshly-starched gowns, the clink of steel against porcelain, the confidential whisper of surgeon to assistant. You sink down into func-

2

tional rubber foam, your hands clasp functional arm rests. You open your mouth and close your eyes. You wait for something to happen. Your palms perspire. Nothing happens. You look up. At the end of the cone of vision there is a face, and on the face there is joy. Out of the lips turned toward you cascades a tingling torrent of happiness. You are being reassured. The condemned man is being given a hearty breakfast.

Catalogue Continued

All of this is what is called public relations, personnel relations, pooh bah. Tax collectors smile, politicians smile when they talk about the budget, flight captains ooze reassurance, even wizened sergeants whose hearts are covered with alligator hide are beginning to talk like the wolf in Little Red Ridinghood.

Which is the point. When as children we read the pitiful story of Ridinghood, the wolf was wicked not merely because he was a wolf but because he was a wolf talking like a kind old woman. And there was the Devil in the Garden. The trouble with the serpent was not that he was a serpent, but that he housed a devil who argued like a god. The wolf oozed reassurance. The serpent oozed reassurance. But they belied facts. Behind their blandness lurked Danger and Death.

The Pedagogic Grin

Quite obviously the sharp edge of reality needs now and then to be blunted. Dentists ought not to glower like ogres.

3

Stewardesses ought not to wail like Antigone going to her death. When children go to the doctor, the whole of reality ought not to be tossed in their lap. But there is grave danger in the other direction also. Much of life is grim, with a grimness which only serious-minded people sustained by grace can confront. The Christian pulpit is a steward of this truth. We do not want gloom pots in our pulpits. But we can do without Happy Harry also. When we ask for the Bread of Life, we don't want to be handed a Chiclet.

The Compleat Angler

Philosophical Fishing

Three hundred years ago a good Christian man by the name of Izaac Walton, whose gift for English prose approached genius, wrote a book called *The Compleat Angler*. It is a leisurely account of the high pleasure of the countryside. After many years of absence from the book, I still retain in my memory its fragrance of English lanes and meadows. Even if Walton's Piscator and Venator and literary mermaids are only creatures of the fancy, they speak the language of enchantment to the heart of the nature enthusiast. It is no sacrilege that sportsmen should have taken the name of Walton for their fraternity, the "Izaak Walton League." He would have approved.

The pleasure of fishing is not limited to the beauty of the setting. It is usually a bad drama which is remembered only for its scenery, and we are never so conscious of the auxiliary pleasures of fishing—the beauty of the clouds, the clean line of the beach, and the blueness of water—as when the fishing luck is poor. The pleasure of fishing is the pleasure of struggle and conquest—the joy of matching wits and strength with an opponent. It is hence a better day when the opponent wins by taking lure and line than when we sit idle with only weed for our consolation. Tennyson was right when he wrote,

> *'Tis better to have loved and lost*
> *Than never to have loved at all.*

Fishing for Keeps

Fishing is an innocent pleasure and, as such, needs no justification. Our old prejudice against diversion which had its roots partly in legalistic piety and partly in an economic concern about wasting time is fortunately vanishing. It is the rare church which begrudges its pastor his vacation; it is the rare individual who does not find some way of relaxing tensions without developing guilt feelings.

Hence it should not be necessary to motivate our fishing expeditions by reference to John 21:3 ("Simon Peter said to them, 'I am going fishing'") as I once heard a minister do. Actually, the fishing about which the New Testament speaks has nothing essential in common with our pleasure fishing except that both are concerned with fish and are carried out on water. It is a bad kind of romanticism which transforms the New Testament into a *Compleat Angler* and thinks of Peter and Andrew as engaged in relaxing sport. But this confusion is part of our larger error about the Bible, viz., that it is a pretty book about lilies and birds and lambs and newly-bathed babies and saintly-looking people attired in something white and freshly laundered. Bethlehem is made into a Christmas card; the crowd around Jesus has no possible resemblance to the ragged, dirty, and sickly throng of undernourished Galilean peasants which must have been His following; we hasten to make Gethsemane into a moonlit trysting place and even the cross, the most vicious and obscene instrument of public torture, is wreathed with lilies.

All this is nonsense, of course. There is beauty in the Bible but it is the beauty of the real world and of real people. Peter and Andrew and the other fishing disciples were commercial fishermen: men who sweated and toiled through the long nights in crude boats with impossible nets. They would have laughed at anyone who suggested the philosophical pleasure of fishing. For them it was what work is for most people: drudgery with rare moments of success or relief.

Fishers of Men

This is the significance also of Jesus' apt metaphor that they are henceforth to be "fishers of men." In the context of pleasure fishing this statement has no meaning at all. For the disciples fishing was a life and death business; you succeeded or you perished. This is the urgency of fishing for men. It is not a sport at which you dabble; it is a work to which you dedicate yourself. Evangelism is not "fun"; it is toil, unremitting and often fruitless toil. It is hence a job for serious-minded people. Such people will recognize their need for diversion, of course. They will not be tiresomely gloomy. But they will understand what many of us do not understand in our day, that our divine commitment is not to play but to service.

Triple Brass

The Dismal Fungus

I see that the journal of Mrs. Robert Louis Stevenson has been found and published. The reviewer of the book takes occasion to speak of Robert Louis Stevenson as "currently out of fashion." It is no doubt true that Stevenson's too conscious art is no longer as popular as once it was. Between his sunny upland and us there is the great gulf of contemporary literature—a gulf filled with the cries of the deranged and the bleat of the self-pitying. But I should think that the man who wrote *Treasure Island* need not worry about his literary immortality. Long after many modern books have been forgotten, Stevenson's novel will speak its enchanting language.

But it is not as a novelist that Stevenson addresses himself to me at the moment but as a will bound with "triple brass." His essay "Aes Triplex" (which is Latin for "triple brass") should speak to anyone who is wearied by all the contemporary talk of safety, security, and prudence. Stevenson calls prudence "dismal fungus."

8

Bubble Gum and
Braces

We are now at the stage of our national development
where we have made a cult of child health. It is not a new
cult, but it is growing stronger. When I was twelve years
old, the subject of hygiene was coming into its own. My
teacher in Health orated about the evils of candy, gum,
Cracker-Jack, pop and all the other pleasant materials of
childhood and had much to say about fruit, vegetables,
morning walks, and digestive regularity. I still recall the
guilt with which my sugar-starved system reacted to this
new Decalogue. I learned to hate my teacher's magnificent
teeth and magnificent complexion, which underscored all
these dismal truths. I was hoping that a champion of childhood would arise and say something in behalf of jawbreak-
ers, ice cream sodas, and all the sovereign gooeyness which
lured me to the Greek chocolate shop. But we kids had no
advocate.

Today we have added to our hypochondria and, what
is most discouraging, our children, their teeth bound with
triple brass, are arguing on the side of toothbrushing and
vitamins. They prefer milk to coffee. Some of the more
advanced disciples have been known to express greater
affection for a head of lettuce than a milk shake. They are
ready at the drop of a hat to give you the precise correlation
between bubble gum and tooth decay.

Tin Shoes and
Tepid Milk

Well, say my Christian friends, what's wrong with all
this? Isn't the body the temple of the Holy Spirit and aren't

we enjoined to care for it? Most assuredly. It is the care-less soldier who does not keep his rifle in order. Our bodies are God's instruments and we are to guard them against wilful neglect and abuse. This is elementary. But we are not just bodies. We are wills too. And while we train our children to wash their hands before eating and to get nine hours of sleep, we ought also to be training them in the fine virtue of courage. I have many times been thankful that St. Paul did not worry too much about his toothbrush, or about getting his feet wet, or about drafts. He must have been the despair of his physician, the good Doctor Luke. "I have been shipwrecked three times. I have been twenty-four hours in the open sea. In my travels I have been in constant danger from rivers and floods, from bandits, from my own countrymen, and from pagans. I have faced danger in city streets, danger in the desert, danger on the high seas, danger among false Christians. I have known exhaustion, pain, long vigils, hunger and thirst, doing without meals, cold and lack of clothing." (Phillips)

Set over against that heroic disregard the fearfulness of an eminent chemist, of whom Stevenson writes that he "took his walks abroad in tin shoes and subsisted wholly upon tepid milk."

"And Gladly Die"

Stevenson himself was a life-long invalid. He tried to regain his health and failed. His body, under the dark pressure of tuberculosis, faded and curled like a fall leaf. But in that fragile casket which was his body there burned, like a fine gem, his imperishable will. A friend once told me that it is better to be a live coward than a dead hero. I don't believe it. I hope I never shall. For to worry about staying alive is not to live at all. And at the end it is to die wormily. With God's help I want to kick off the tin shoes and dash the mug of lukewarm milk to the ground. I want to live with hazard. I want a heart bound with triple brass. It would be good to say some day with the dying Robert Louis,

> *Under the wide and starry sky*
> *Dig the grave and let me die;*
> *Glad did I live and gladly die,*
> *And I laid me down with a will.*

Psychiatry and Faith

Religion and the Egg-Heads

The amount of religious interest in our common life in America no longer surprises us. We take pretty much for granted a strong popular response to the Peales, the Sheens, and the Grahams. What is more surprising is the growing awareness of religious faith among the "long-haired," i.e., the arty and the intellectual.

In a May issue of the *New Republic* there is, for example, a long discussion of psychiatry and faith. The main article, "Analysis and Faith," written by William H. Roberts, a professor of psychology, is followed by a series of comments by prominent psychiatrists and clergymen. Even Carl Jung gets into the act.

In any resurgence of faith there is inevitably confusion of judgment. Paul had trouble with disorderliness in the Corinthian church. In the high tides of medieval piety some refused to eat milk and eggs and others danced naked through the village streets. The Reformation had Munster with its forced baptisms and polygamy. In our own day we find amazing naiveté in religious matters among many people. It is not uncommon to find the same person an enthusiastic devotee of both Bishop Sheen and Billy Graham.

Freud and
Faith

But what is forgivable among the uncritical is less excusable among those who make it a business to be scientific. And in few areas is there more confusion than in the relation of faith to mental health. Typical of this confusion is one of Dr. Roberts' sentences which I shall make the text of my brief exhortation:

> "More and more the analyses of the problems that torment men, women, and children and the solutions that psychologists offer, are coming to resemble those proposed by priests and theologians."

This is a fairly common opinion. It forms the basis for many articles in popular and semi-scholarly journals. Unfortunately, it does justice neither to psychiatry nor to theology.

Drawing a line between psychiatry and faith does not mean that the two are in any way competitive. What it does mean is that the two operate in different worlds. The task of the psychiatrist is to restore his patient to the emotional and psychic balance which will permit some sort of "normal" functioning. There may, of course, be religious factors in the solution of the emotional problem. If so, the skilful psychiatrist, even though he may put no faith in objective spiritual reality as such, will take such factors into account. But I believe that it is possible to be a good

13

psychiatrist, as it is possible to be a skilled surgeon, without being committed to religious faith.

The reason for this is that, like any other scientist, the psychiatrist works within the realm of human experience, which may be scientifically observed. He may be aware of the need of religious faith and he may even direct his patient toward such a faith in the interest of mental health, but if he does this, his aim is not religious but scientific. He prescribes religion as a physician might prescribe an antibiotic.

The Field of the Minister

The theologian or minister, unlike the psychiatrist, is not primarily interested in harmonious emotional adjustment. For the minister the aim of all activity is salvation. And salvation is a matter of ultimate standing before God. Now the experience of the new birth often results in a more harmonious inner life just as transgression is frequently the cause of mental disturbance. Furthermore it is certainly the Christian's responsibility to guard his emotional health as well as that of others. By creating the sort of emotional climate which will fortify rather than destroy mental health the Christian enters into the ministry of healing in an even more significant way than by attending only to the needs of the body. But having said this, we must insist that salvation is more than health and well-being. God's mercy extends not only to the dull-witted and the idiotic but in a significant way also to the deranged.

The Golden Horn

He Should Have Died
Hereafter

We are never quite ready for death. When news is brought to Macbeth that his queen has died, he says

She should have died hereafter;
There would have been time for such a word.

Many must have felt that about the death of Homer Allan Rodeheaver. He had been something in himself, and he stood for something in the spiritual tradition of America. I saw and heard him one memorable day at Northfield, Mass., many years ago. I remember the white flannels and blue coat and the gold trombone. I remember the grace with which he made people sing. The grace and the joy. I was a high school boy, a little ashamed of the tackiness of the faith. I had been reading Sinclair Lewis and Theodore Dreiser. My faith seemed dismal; light filtered through a sooty pane; sound adenoidal and tremulous. Then I heard Homer Rodeheaver. The same day I saw G. Campbell Morgan and a wonderful little Englishman named Hutton. But it was the golden horn that did it. It enriched the faith. "He should have died hereafter. There would have been a time for such a word."

What we want, I suppose, is unending enrichment. We want to be surrounded by everybody. We want to see tier upon tier of people about us: the very old, the middle-aged, the young. We want nothing to be diminished. We fear growing poorer—to be unclothed. We do not want the years to deprive us; we are hoping that this new year will cram us with blessings; more blessings, bigger blessings. And all this is so because we do not believe in heaven any more. Or we do not understand it.

Nobody's Talking About Heb'n

We were a group of good friends around a restaurant table just before Christmas. One of the men said to me, "Why don't you say something about heaven in your column? Or don't we believe in heaven any more?" I don't know. What I do know is that good Christian people are beginning to think of death as the supreme evil. If they accept heaven at all, they do it with the reluctance which they manifest on going to the hospital for major surgery or on leaving for the county poor farm. That is why even good Christians are being given nembutal or codeine before plunging into the river of death; it seems easier to snuffle one's way into the kingdom of joy.

For Me to Die

What is it to die? From one point of view it is the great privation, *the great divorce* of C. S. Lewis. It is the child being dragged reluctantly to bed from his train and Erector set. It is to be unclothed. Honors, dignities, powers, responsibilities drop away. The thread of coherence melts, and the structure of the flesh once glorying in its glory sinks and crumbles. The soul immersed in the thick relationships of other souls is nudged away from the center of things and lives like King Lear without kingdom and without retinue. The great Loneliness begins. All this it is to die.

Gain

But this is not all. There enters upon this thin darkness not merely a new planet or a new galaxy but a new Universe. It breaks in upon us in the midst of our poverty and our loneliness. "The people who sit in darkness shall see a great light." Its character is light. That truth speaks in Genesis, in 1 John, and in the Revelation. The kingdom of heaven is the unbroken and unfettered flowing of light from Him who is the father of lights. But it is more than incandescence. It is victory. The struggle against the darkness is dramatic. Heaven is not boredom. There are harps, but they do not strum idly. They also share in the struggle of the light. In the midst of the music there is risk. And the light is personal. It is not cold wattage. The life is the light of men. In the midst of heaven there is the Lamb that was slain, and the Lamb is the light of the city. And all around the Lamb, tier upon tier, rank upon rank, are the clouds of witnesses. This is the final enrichment. And if I may be forgiven a bit of whimsy, there too is the golden horn of Homer Rodeheaver.

Hence we speak not with Macbeth but with the Apostle Paul these first days of the New Year, "for me to live is Christ, and to die is gain."

17

The Enriching Detour

The Long Way
Around

Charles R. Brown of Yale once preached a sermon on the wilderness wanderings of the Israelites which he called "The Long Way Around." In it he told about the way in which God enriched the people of Israel by keeping them circling around for forty years in the wilderness. The idea falls with a grating sound on our modern ears. We are in the grip of the conviction that if we move fast we shall have more time when we get there. If we can get the day's work over in eight hours or four, we shall have more time to tinker with our souls.

Seaweed Mignon

A commentator we picked up on the car radio while driving north was sneering at the antiquated methods of feeding the human race. Cows eat grass, he said. Then we drink the cow's milk. Or we eat the cow. This is a waste of time and energy. Why not omit the middleman and eat

18

the grass directly. It is obviously more nourishing than either milk or cow.

Row, Row, Row
Your Boat

Even the northland is dedicated to speed. It is considered old-fashioned to row a boat in pursuit of fish. You rent a motorized boat or you rent a rowboat and use your own motor. In this way you can cover more water and get more fish. And presumably have more fun. We rented a rowboat and toiled at the oars. When the other boats roared past our antiquated craft, we felt as an Amish farmer must feel when his horse-drawn buggy is passed by 260 horsepower of pastelled steel.

The Hare and the
Tortoise

But the old fable is right. The tortoise gets to the destination ahead of the hare. To shorten time is to impoverish it. To move too fast is to push life back on either side and to live in emptiness. We hit a detour between Portal, N. D., and Regina, Sask. It led us out into the prairie. The road was a dirt track following section lines. But all at once we saw the sky in its blue vastness overhead, and as we slowed down we saw sloughs and marshes alive with water birds. After a while we were barely crawling, and finally we stopped. The fever of speed was washed out of our blood. The wind came back and was our friend again. The scent of the fields was ours. We saw flowers and grasses very near. We were gripped by a love of the land.

I remembered a trip I had made three weeks before from San Francisco to Chicago in a Super G Constellation with a cruising speed of 365 miles per hour. We travelled at 21,000 feet. The country below looked like a grayish contour map. The great Salt Lake was the size of a puddle. Denver was a lighted blur. Thus speed impoverishes.

You Can't Go Home Again

Now no one but a romantic would imagine that people will choose to turn the clock back. After struggling with a wood stove, an old-fashioned icebox, and an outdoor powder room here at the lake, you begin to think about all the conveniences you had back in Chicago. And you are thankful for technology.

The point is not that we should stop technological progress. This cannot be done. The point is that we should realize how much every technological advance is costing us in inner wealth. I pity the man who has never had to row to a fishing spot, who has never had to walk farther than to his garage, who has never felt the indescribable thrill of a roaring wood fire in a cold cabin. I pity the child who has never had to manufacture his own toys or find his own diversion in woods and fields because technology and wealth have done the job for him. I pity people if they believe that God does not bless except in the heart of a twentieth century city. I believe in God's long way around, and sometimes I am lonesome for it as the lucky Israelites must have been after they got to the land of milk and honey.

The Glass of Fashion

Hats

Nonconformity is supposed to be an American virtue, but even those who talk loudest about it sneak a look now and then at the glass of fashion. Ralph Waldo Emerson wrote impassioned essays about self-reliance, but his cravat seems to have been well ordered when he sat for his tintype. My own faith in nonconformity has been tested recently by the gift of a hat. Unfortunately a gift of this type has got to be worn. There are ways of concealing other gifts. A bad picture can be hung in the broom closet. A poor book can get lost on your shelves. A doorstop can do good service in obscurity. But a hat has got to be worn. In public.

The Mad Hatter

My hat came from a respectable haberdasher in Stockholm, Paul U. Bergstrom, and the trademark PUB is supposed to mean that the product can be worn with perfect assurance among civilized people. It is true that the crown was low and the brim narrow and that the material was not felt but tweed. But spurred by the urgings of my friends and an innate contempt for mere imitation, I decided to wear the thing downtown. As someone said, "If Sherlock Holmes could get by with wearing that kind of hat, why can't you?"

Don Quixote on State Street

The illusion of normalcy lasted until I parked my car south of the Loop and headed north on State Street. It was glorious winter weather; the Christmas rush was over, and people were out to exchange their gifts and to pick up bargains. I walked like a man with an objective, unaware that I was stopping traffic. It was only when I came to a red light at the corner of Jackson and State that I realized that my hat had become a rock of offense. A very large man behind me made a profane comment about my little hat to his girl friend. (His own head was covered by a ruin, but it was the right kind of ruin.) There was a tinkle of laughter. A silver tinkle.

For a moment my courage failed me. I wanted to retreat. I thought of slipping into an alley and cramming the offending hat into my pocket. But then history helped me. I thought of Diogenes in his cask. I thought of Carrie Nation. The unswerving. And I pushed on.

Hats Off

My nonconformist hat is off to those who do not yield readily to every pressure of fashion. I honor those who dare to have a picture window without a flocked tree, green glass balls, and a spotlight; those men who do not have a single pink and charcoal item in their wardrobe; those who do not ship off all their ugly and outmoded furniture to their summer cottage but leave a few pieces around out of sentiment; those who still kneel by their beds when they pray; those who dare to have Scripture mottoes on their walls; those who can read the Bible without feeling self-conscious. I also congratulate those who hang very modern paintings on their walls and who furnish their homes with chairs that look like clam shells balanced on tooth picks, *if that's the way they want it.*

Conformity and Transformation

Nonconformity is good, but there is something better. America needs people who are honestly different. It needs tweed hats and togas and bast shoes. But to be different is not always to be right. In the first centuries Christian women wore white as a protest against the riotous color of pagan fashions. They wore veils in public. They did not curl their hair or use cosmetics or wear fancy shoes. Christian men did not curl their beards or wear pomade. In all this they were nonconformists. But if they had been only that, they would not have made a dent. Rome was full of more exciting species of differentness than the Christian. The dent was made by people who had "let God remould their minds from within." (Phillips). This transformation was the ground of nonconformity. The humility, the gratitude, and the shyness which grace imparted was the real protest against the pride, the hardness, and the insolence of the Roman world. It was the freshly laundered soul rather than the severely tailored toga which turned the tide for Christendom.

The Slaughter of the Innocents

Ding Dong

December 28 is the Feast of the Holy Innocents in the church calendar. It commemorates the slaughter of the children of Bethlehem by Herod as recorded by St. Matthew. It has made me ask what our time is doing to our children.

Herod the Great was not a nice man. The Emperor Augustus, who wasn't virtuous himself, said he would rather be Herod's pig than his son. Josephus gives us a much more detailed picture than Matthew of the old tyrant. It is not pretty.

What, you may ask, can lead the mind from Herod to our time? Look at all we do for our children: the vitamins, the vaccines, the ventilation. Look at the Frankness with which we give them the Facts. Look at the thoroughly practical nature of our education. Look at the Quiz Kids. Look at Ding Dong School.

Visibility Zero

We may as well begin with Ding Dong School. It looks innocent enough: the kindly, ample lady who smiles at our

24

moppets from the TV screen and helps to shape their vocabulary and their ideas. What could be sweeter and gentler? Her stories have no plot to knot little foreheads and set little hearts to beating faster. Her schoolroom does not suggest the dark and the perplexing. All is fair weather and friendly fun.

I grew up in the midst of superstition. My home was free of it, but what I didn't get at home, I got in rich measure from the Skåne farmers and their children. The forest was full of nonhuman creatures: hairy trolls, brownies, whirling bands of elves in the August moonlight, the river god with his enchanting fiddle, and serried ranks of ghosts from our Viking ancestors down to the village lunatic who hanged himself in a woodshed just last year. But nothing intrigued and frightened us quite so much as the elfmaid *(skogsrå)*. She was surpassingly beautiful from the front, but her back was hollowed out like a decayed tree. She lured the lonely traveler with promises of food and shelter, but if he followed she shut him up forever in her mountain dwelling.

The Hollow Man

Much of modern education is learning without dimension. When it turns its back, the sickening hollowness is seen. And it is hollow because it has no theology of childhood. It does not look upon the child as a creature both involved in and on the verge of being involved in the perplexity of sin. It has no concept of innocence since innocence is always related to moral risk. It thinks of the child as a spiritual neutral. Hence it is unprepared for the ugliness which threatens and often emerges in the life of the child: the cruelty, the rampant selfishness, the deviousness, the pride. When these traits appear in the child, the educator takes refuge in psychological explanations which evade the issue of right and wrong, bad and good. Or if the child's behavior reaches a truly serious stage, as in the case of juvenile delinquents, the blame is readily shifted to parents. The glib ultimatum is delivered, "There are no juvenile delinquents; there are only adult delinquents." The really difficult question remains: When does the child who does not sin become the adult who sins not only in himself but through his child?

China Dolls With Grown-Up Faces

I recently saw an exhibit of dolls from a century ago. The striking thing about them was that they all had the faces of old children or adults. In the exhibit there wasn't a single "baby doll." If modern education errs on the side of treating the child as if he had no responsibility for his acts, the evangelical churches have erred in the opposite direction. They also have been deficient in a theology of childhood. The dolls have had grown-up faces. The activity known as "child evangelism" has used techniques adapted to the child's interest level, but has often assumed that a child is an adult both in the matter of his sin and in his experience of grace. Now a child is a sinner, but he is this in his own way. And the child needs grace, but he needs a grace that is related to his sin. If we do not understand this, we impose on the child an unreal experience of sinfulness (our experience) and an unreal experience of grace. The child will imitate us in his actions and in his speech. He will embrace our vocabulary. But if it is not *his* experience expressed in *his* words, he may grow up to reject what we cherish for him.

When We Were Very Young

Mencken and Milne

Death came this month to two men of letters whose most avid readers had been the very young. They were H. L. Mencken and A. A. Milne. Mencken did not compose verse for children and his name will be remembered, if at all, for his vast studies of the American language. But even though he never spoke, as Milne, to toy-strewn floors and clown-figured wall paper, Mencken also addressed himself to children. In the post World War I era he was the spokesman for the emotional infants who had thrown away their horns and had bought hammers. He was the patron saint of the nursery rebel and the debunker. With George Jean Nathan he put on the Titanic Tantrum, to the distress of all the jolly babies in the nursery who wanted to be good children.

The American Mercury

From 1924 to 1933 Mencken was editor of the old *American Mercury*, which has about as much resemblance to the current periodical as a Bengal tiger to a tabby. In its pages all forms of restraint were clawed. Mencken flayed William Jennings Bryan; he hooted at prohibition; he jeered and snarled at every sacred American convention, from Saturday night baths to revival meetings. Together with Theodore Dreiser and Sinclair Lewis he was held up by many American Christians as Antichrist, the defiler of the sanctuary.

I first learned of Mencken from the village agnostic in my home town. He was my employer, and from the tender age of 12 until I had finished high school I was treated almost daily to a diet of Mencken, H. G. Wells, George Jean Nathan, Marcus Aurelius, Nietzsche, and a woman named Vina Delmar. (The *i* in her name had a serpentine mark over it which made it peculiarly foreign and sinister. I remember that.) Toward all of these people I had a "double" attitude. On the one hand they repelled me. They were so unlike the good people I knew: the solid, unpretentious, Swedish immigrants in whose midst I lived. They were so different from my family circle, the integrity of which I did not question.

But, on the other hand, I realized that much of what they said was true. It did not take unusual powers of observation to identify Lincoln Avenue in my home town with Sinclair Lewis' *Main Street*. And midway in my high school career I had met enough Elmer Gantries and Sharon Falconers to be convinced that the shriek which rose from the church was not so much the outcry of insulted innocence as the protest of exposed weakness. The church of the 1920's was sanctified respectability. It lost its hold on people because it rested on its ornately carved sarcophagus, an effigy in stone. It existed within the sacred circle of

28

blue: the blue law, the blue light of the police station, and the blue nose. It needed to be laughed at, and God in his infinite mercy permitted the laugh.

Mercurial
Laughter

Now nearly all the great troubling spirits have left the scene. Dreiser is dead. And Lewis. And Mencken. They were good for America but not good enough. They laughed and screamed but not always at the right things. Their gripe was indiscriminate. Against all three the same charge can be made: They lacked structure. To the question: But what is it you really want? they had no answer. It is one thing to shriek out our revulsion against all things which check and harry us. Like a child in a snugglebunny or a pig in a poke. It is quite another to direct men to the land of peace.

The Birth from
Above

Some years ago I was discussing St. Augustine with a man who had translated the *Confessions* into Swedish. He said, "Augustine was only a second-rate writer before he became a Christian." Just this month we have been given the story of the conversion of C. S. Lewis in his book *Surprised by Joy*. It tells of the recreative impact of the Christian faith upon his life and thought. What is true of C. S. Lewis was true of Dante. He could not have written the *Divine Comedy* without the New Life. We are led to wonder what might have happened to the bright and bitter talent of the twenties if it too had been converted and baptized.

Vitamins and the Way of Life

Birdseed and Blessing

A few weeks ago I heard a radio interview with a prominent Broadway personality. This was a lady, and after giving us, in a fruity voice, the usual chitchat about Manhattan, "show business," and all the darling people everywhere, she gave a personal testimony about her diet. It turned out that she was a vegetarian. I want to make clear from the start what people eat is strictly their own business. I heard of a man once who ate only bananas. It sounds monotonous, but it is not unconstitutional. The stomach is such a subtle organ and is so intimately related to the well-being of the whole bodily republic that a man should be permitted to make peace with it on any and all terms.

What nettled me about the Broadway lady was that, after she had made her confession, she dropped her voice a half octave and gave the whole thing a religious dimension. It wasn't that the unadorned carrot and slippery birdseed rustling against the heap of breakfast timothy gave her more physical pep. Oh no! Black strap molasses, slivered avocados, raw sugar, and unsweetened grapefruit juice were a way of salvation. "It lifts my spirits," she said. "I think it makes me a better person."

The Adorable Artichoke

Some may feel that I am exaggerating, but a personal encounter with a vegetarian will soon dispel this notion. The devoted lover of herbage is not lukewarm about his lima beans. He loves them as strenuously as he hates anything meaty. To him the mousy, gray-collar worker munching his way through meat loaf is as much a cannibal as the African aborigine. He wears the brand of Cain. Recently in Europe a group of vegetarians made a test pilgrimage to see how far they could walk without food or water. And they did it with the religious enthusiasm of Christians going to the lions, or medieval almoners trudging toward the Savior's tomb.

The Body and the Soul

There is, of course, a connection between the body and the soul. The spiritual man will order his entire life according to the urgings of the Holy Ghost. His body is a temple of the Spirit. But this is a sanctification from above; it is not idolatry from below. It is one thing to avoid gluttony because I am a spiritual person; it is quite another to believe that I am a religious person because I gnaw mournfully at a raw turnip.

Litany of
Laughter

But the vegetarians are not alone. Recently I heard
of an organization called something like Laughter Incorporated. It discovers and trains laughers. There is a practical
angle to this. TV and radio needs strategically placed laughers. You can put a laugh on tape and splice it in when
the audience reaction indicates lowered barometric pressure. So far so good. Let us not begrudge the harassed TV
industry its consolation. Perhaps laughter can be carbonated
and sold by the case for people who have trouble laugh-
ing at the right places. You could keep it on ice. Bottled
Horse Laughs. Grins and Titters. Giggles.

But it is quite another matter when laughter is made
into a gospel. Laughter Incorporated gave us, after a duet
of shrieks by two amateur laughers about to turn professional, a serious discourse on the Benefit of Laughter.
It was terrifying. Laughter turned out to be good for the
digestion, for family living, and for international relations. If only more people would laugh systematically
and religiously, this would be a better world. So ran the
argument.

The Olympics and
Geo-Politics

This trend toward making everything a religion has also
invaded the Olympics. It is not only the pageantry—the
sacred torch, the colorful vestments of the participants—
that point in this direction. It is the talk. We are now
risking life and limb on the bobsled and slalom runs, not
because such sport is an invigorating kind of insanity with-

out any practical purpose but because there are Beefy Bolsheviks whose muscular excellence challenges our way of life. To lose out to the Commies on the dirt track is to betray not only the Stars and Stripes but Western Christendom. I don't want to sound irreverent, but I question if Heaven will wait with bated breath this summer for the running of the 1,000 meter event. It is not the Battle of Armageddon.

The Bitter Pleasure

Early to
Bed

Some time during the reign of Septimius Severus when the Christians in North Africa were having a bad time, Quintus Septimius Florens Tertullianus wrote to his wife advising her against a second marriage in the event he should die. His letter, which has little good to say about marriage, speaks about the "bitter, bitter pleasure of children." Tertullian was thinking of what happened to babies when they were thrown to the wild cows and the hungry bears of the Carthaginian arena or when they were left orphaned by the persecutions. I thought of the phrase "bitter pleasure" when I stood a few days ago in the cemetery in Paxton, Illinois. There were three small headstones in marble. The inscriptions were barely legible. The rain and the snows had touched them with gentleness. Only the names and the dates remained. The poetry had vanished like an old grief. There was Carie May Mc Cracken who died January 3, 1871. She was three. Then there was her five-year-old sister, Helen Addie. Helen died on January 9. There was a girl of seven named Alice Cecelia. She lived until January 24. Three McCracken girls dead in three weeks. And they were not alone. In 1879 the Swansons lost a child in each of the three winter months: January, February, and March.

We are sometimes critical of Victorian sentimentality. I have said some harsh words myself about the "cult of the death bed"—the weeping willow, the stringless lute, the empty chair, the baggage car ahead. But when you come face to face with the reality, the bravado withers. In the nineteenth century people had a lot to say about death because they lived in its presence. Let us admit that much of what they said was poorly stated. It was ornate, hollow, and trite. But if it sustained the grieving, may peace attend it and them!

Operation Iodoform

When I was seven, our family was stricken with measles. It was in the gray years after World War I in Europe, and undernourishment prepared the way for all sorts of complications. Within a few weeks both my sister and I landed in the Provincial Hospital in southern Sweden, she with mastoiditis and I with some sort of undetermined infection of the arm. Proust has told us with variations how evocative of things past are certain scents and tastes. I bear him witness. The odor of iodoform transplants me into a children's ward of that old hospital; the beds range themselves side by side in a geography of pain. I was brought in shaking with chills and flushed with fever. It was Saturday night. My bed was in the northeast corner. Only the night lights burned. I had parted from my mother

35

a few minutes before. All around me in the antiseptic murk there were small moans. I was sure that I was going to die. My soul moved inward from the unwieldy outwardness which was my body. I heard the rustle of a starched dress. A soft voice said, "I am sister Martha." And then in the polite manner in which children are addressed in that country, "Karl trusts in Jesus. He is not afraid to die, is he?" I was somewhere in and down, and I remember feeling very solemn about the question. But then, at that moment, I do not recall feeling afraid. What I felt was the sort of resignation which, I am sure, is not uncommon in children. I was resigned about earth. This is the way it was: sickness, insecurity, sadness. Ultimately there was death. Sooner or later you had to make a pilgrimage inward from the body, which skated and swam and ran and hungered and which now shook and roared with sickness. That wasn't the end. But it was the beginning of something different.

Makes a Man
Wise

In the gray winter light which filtered in through the windows the following morning I saw the island of misery on which I had been thrown. Some day I shall have to recall my neighbors. Most of them suffered from surgical tuberculosis: their earthly future was bleak. Now all I shall recall is my rapid recovery and the way in which with every hour of returning health my will to live increased. I remember my last afternoon at the hospital before I was to return home. It was early sunset with the rosy light falling sadly on a facade opposite the window where I stood. I was gripped with fear. Now in the moment of my returning to life, I did not want to die. I felt almost resentful toward my friends of the ward because they suggested death to me. What did I have to do with them? And yet I knew then in my childish heart that my day of reckoning was not cancelled. It was merely postponed. Who knows? Perhaps I envied them a little who still faced inward—who were destined to go "early to bed."

The Integration of Islam

What's the Difference?

During the past week I had two inter-faith experiences: I went to the Bas Mitzvah of the daughter of a friend of mine who is a Jewish Rabbi, and I heard a round-table discussion on how to get along with Islam. The Bas Mitzvah, the parallel service to the Bar Mitzvah which makes a Jewish boy of 13 a "son of the commandment," was simple and beautiful. The rabbi's daughter read a long passage in Hebrew and gave a brief address in English. She then received her father's blessing. He prayed for her that she might become a Sarah, a Rebecca, a Rachel, and a Leah —a good wife and mother of Israel. It was very moving. It was also saddening. Because no matter how much my Jewish friend and I have in common: the Old Testament Scriptures, the Judaeo-Christian ethical tradition, the value-system of the Western world, we do not share the most precious thing of all—a common faith. He is a Jew; I am a Christian. It makes a lot of difference.

Efforts to obliterate this difference in the interest of

"community" strike me as being particularly silly. We have every reason in the world to live together as neighbors. I value my Jewish friends, I rejoice in our common convictions on ethical and social questions, I appreciate their intellectual and artistic sensitivity. I think that every effort to block the Jews or any other minority group from a full share of the blessings of America is vicious and stupid: vicious because it violates our own system of values; stupid because oppression deprives us of the spiritual treasures of a truly integrated society.

But having said this, I cannot go on to minimize the things which keep us apart. This was the procedure of the Christian and Moslem to whose radio round-table I refer.

Mohammed and Monotheism

For some obscure reason, known only to those who organize events of this type, the entire evening was devoted to showing that the differences between Christian and Moslem were mere soap bubbles. Christians and Mohammedans both believe in a "spiritual" view of the universe, which means, we were told, that they both believe in the same God to whom men are responsible. They believe in an afterlife of rewards and punishments. The Koran makes room for Jesus as a prophet. The imagery of the Koran about heaven—the garden and the damsels and all that —is not intended to be taken literally, said the Moslem. But now the Christian was chortling with enthusiasm. "We have our crude images too," he confessed; "that business of the golden streets and the harps." The summation seemed to indicate that Christ and Mohammed, Bible and Koran, mosque and church were only variations on the same grand theme. I expected the two brothers in the faith to close by singing together, "When we all get to heaven, what a day of rejoicing that will be."

Fly in the Petroleum

At some point during this mellifluous exchange of pleasantries, the radio announcer suggested that perhaps the Jews belong here also. Weren't they monotheists? The Christian brother who had been soaring higher and higher on the pinion of his zeal for Islamic civilization, came down with a thud. So did the Mussulman. After all, *this* was the committee for Muslim-Christian friendship. The committee's work should not be complicated by asking it to be friendly also to the Jews. In some future aeon it might be possible to include the Jews, but right now . . . well, it was just out of the question. That distressing business in Palestine, for example.

Oil of Gladness

I should like to make clear that I believe in lubricating the creaking machinery of international relations. We need the Mohammedans and they need us. We need to make friends and to influence people. So do they. Let us get to work as soon as possible on understanding them and their contribution to our culture. Let us carry on a conversation about common areas of interest, and let us even include theology in that conversation. But let us not sell our birthright and our blessing for the sake of international lentil soup. To me, as a Christian, Christ is not "about the same thing" as Mohammed. He is my Savior and Lord. The nonpolitical Moslem will understand what I mean.

The Little Foxes

Annoyance

There ought to be a doctrine about irritation. Something helpful should be said about mosquitoes and chigger bites. I am not sure about Job's boils. Should they be treated as a major or a minor suffering? Dante has an assortment of discomforts in "The Inferno": rain, hail, snow, smells, but they are so numerous that the effect is entirely serious. They constitute suffering, not annoyance. I am thinking about an eyelash or a fleck of soap in the eye, paint running down into your cuff when you are painting a ceiling, smoke in your face as you are stoking a camp fire and the wind veers, running out of gas, a shower of drops inside your collar when you walk under a wet tree, a shovel trying to pick up gravel from a sidewalk, a piece of impure chalk which screeches against a blackboard, a torn fingernail catching in wool. None of these things are worthy of the name of suffering, but I sometimes wonder if they do not call for a larger measure of patience than the big pains.

Tender Grapes

"Our vines have tender grapes," says the Song of Solomon. We are, alas, tender-skinned. Fatigue adds to our sensitivity; so does worry. But even when we are fully rested and under no particular strain there are things which rob us of our cheer. Among the little foxes who ravage our tender grapes, no fox is foxier, more pointed of snout and sharper of claw than the Habitual Corrector. Now correction is good and we ought to receive it with gravity and meekness, but it is so excruciatingly painful that it should be administered only by a loving hand. Our kith and kin, brimming with tenderness, should be the source of our chastening, not the cold stranger. The man who goes around looking for faults simply because he enjoys correcting them is not a major villain. He is no Lucifer or Judas Iscariot. He shouldn't kid himself. But he is a small pain.

Small Foxes and Little Grapes

It is characteristic of the vulpine (from the Latin *vulpes,* meaning fox) personality that it is drawn to the small grapes. The little fox does not attack your philosophy or your taste; he deals with pronunciation, grammatical detail, incidental facts. He is the sort of person who sits watching you with a hard eye and a sensitive nose; he can scent a split infinitive at 500 yards; a hesitation about *who* and *whom* sends him into gluffing transports. He likes to correct anecdotes. You are just rounding the bend of a story and are coming into the home stretch. This is going to be good, you feel. Real good. And in the dramatic silence the fox bays. "Listen, Joe," he says, "that isn't the way it was. Don't you remember that it's the deacon and not the preacher who makes the comment. You're spoiling the point."

Teeth Set
on Edge

The little fox specializes in facts, raw facts. He knows the names of all of the wives of Henry VIII, he knows that the Declaration of Independence was not originally called that; he knows the difference between the 18th Amendment and the Volstead Act. And he punctures all the little pleasant legends: the Dutch boy with his finger in the dike, Washington and the cherry tree, the tradition of Honest Abe.

There is, of course, nothing wrong with stuffing your mind full of all these facts. It may serve on a quiz program. The wrong lies in using your knowledge to expose the ignorance of others.

Sour Grapes

Why are people fond of correcting others? Why do the foxes ravage the tender grapes? Our friend the little fox does what he does because he is hungry. A feeling of emptiness gnaws at his inwards. He wants what he can't have. "A critic," said someone in the 18th century, "is a poet who has failed." A fox may be someone who has wanted very much to be human but could only be a fox.

43

The House of Christmas

The Place Where God Was Homeless

Gilbert Keith Chesterton, who put paradoxes into everything he wrote, has written some lines about Christmas in which the same fondness for contradiction appears. The poem is called "The House of Christmas."

> There fared a mother driven forth
> Out of an inn to roam;
> In the place where she was homeless
> All men are at home.

It is a curious fact that Christmas, which is such a home festival and in which we remember, albeit reluctantly, even those kinsmen we have ignored for a twelvemonth—it is a curious fact that Christmas began in homelessness. Joseph and Mary went away from home to celebrate the first Christmas. Our Christmas card stable looks very cozy: the beasts are clean and well-mannered, Joseph has put on a fresh shirt, and Mary looks unlike any mother who ever arose from childbed. But this is myth-making.

44

We cannot stand to have the stable look inhospitable or strange. There must be geraniums at the window and the faint odor of the percolator—then we can accept the Bethlehem pilgrimage. But the reality is something else: "There was no room for them in the inn."

This, It Is Triste

With a bitter-sweet taste I remember Christmas 1944. It was at the very peak of Rundstedt's desperate bid for a break-through to the channel ports. Our task force had been sent to fight a delaying action on the eastern banks of the Meuse River. If the offensive got too hot, we were to roll back across the Meuse bridges and blow them before German armor could reach them. It was Christmas Eve. We had just crawled across the heavily-mined bridges and were waiting in column for the move into defensive positions. The sun was setting in a clear sky. There was no snow but hard frost, and the road rang underfoot. Toward us in the growing dusk came an unending procession of civilians. We had seen them all day, with bundles on their backs, or trundling baby buggies, or pushing spindly carts. For the third time in a lifetime they were fleeing from German armies. A middle-aged woman came up to my jeep and paused for a moment to rest. Wanting to communicate in some way with her despair, I said a few words in schoolbook French. She was Flemish; and my accent must have made her think that I was trying to talk English. After two or three tries, I finally succeeded in getting my condolence across. "Yes," she said, "this, it is triste (sad) on Christmas Eve." She said it tearlessly as if the luxury of tears lay far behind her. I remember the weariness in her voice. In her own way she had entered into the mysterious homelessness which is the heart of Christmas.

Home Shall Men Come

There is another incident just as real. A shy soldier came to me near Zwolle in Louisiana in August, 1943, and said quite simply, "I would like to find my family." He had been left in an orphanage at the age of three. At 12 he had left the institution in the company of an older brother. They had found work with a farmer. Some months later the older brother was taken to the hospital with appendicitis. During his convalescence the ceiling in his hospital room caved in, and he was killed. Since then, the soldier had had no family. When other men crowded around the postal clerk at mail call, he had nothing to wait for.

Together we did a little detective work. Fortunately, he remembered the name of the orphanage. The orphanage had been closed for many years, but the records had been retained. Thus we got the name of the boy's home town. It was on Long Island. The postmaster was obliging. He wrote at once and said that the father was still living in the town. The suspense grew. If the boy wrote, what would be the answer? We took the chance. In a few days a letter came back from the father. It was written in a shaky hand, but the message was unmistakable, "This is still your home." The company commander cooperated with a furlough. When the soldier arrived at home, the whole family had gathered from Virginia and Florida.

There were brothers and sisters and nieces and nephews. There were gifts, dinners, picnics. It was like a page out of Dickens.

At the expiration of the furlough, the shy soldier came in to see me. He wanted to thank me, but more than anything else he wanted to show me that he belonged. Out of his pocket came a new billfold stuffed with snapshots. "This is my half-brother Wilbur and his wife and their collie. And this is my dad. And here's one of my nieces, Kathie; she's real cute."

"It must have been nice to get home," I said.

"Yes," he said, "it was wonderful. And you know, Chaplain, they all wanted me—it was like I'd never gone away."

And this too is the heart of Christmas.

The Golden Fleece

What Price Beauty?

Haircuts in Chicago are now $1.75 on normal days and $2.00 if you are forgetful, that is, on Saturdays or before holidays. That's a lot of money for a haircut. I wonder how long it will take the barbers' union or whoever decides these things to realize that even in the technically difficult skill of haircutting it is possible to price yourself out of a market. I do not intend to attack the profession of barbering. It is an old and honorable profession. People have always had hair; hair grows; the average person cannot cut his hair without help. There are gadgets on the market which are supposed to help you cut your own hair with the aid of a mirror, but the results are not encouraging. This situation and probably the shortage of applicants for the job of barbering have led to the latest reckless measure.

Hair and
Xenophon

Perhaps the situation will be bearable for those who get something more than a shearing for their money. I have always been fortunate in this respect. I have a Greek friend who used to read Xenophon's *Anabasis* to me in the purest Attic while he was trimming my sideburns. But if the present trend continues, not even a Great Books course with your neck trim will do much good. More and more people are going to call upon the family to help them get their hair cut. This counteraction is already under way. The results so far are mediocre, but I predict that this will not matter. Even if the American male begins to look like the double-crested cormorant, he will prefer domestic barbering to a professional fleecing.

Hair and
Housing

What is true in barbering has been true in housing since the end of World War II. A great deal of the steam behind the present do-it-yourself movement in American building was the disgust generated in the minds of returning servicemen. They found themselves priced out of housing through exorbitant and illegal rent demands and out of building by antiquated codes and impossible construction costs. And so, for better or for worse and because this is still a free country, they did things for themselves.

There have been mishaps. There was the night that I went to work on an unmanageable faucet. Something went terribly wrong and a very kind union plumber had

49

to come in after working hours to save us. He acted calm, professional, and not too condescending. And to my embarrassment he sent a very small bill.

But though there are minor casualties, the trend in American life is unmistakable. Like a mighty army the people are fighting mounting costs with margarine, powdered milk, and wallboard.

Something in the Woodpile

There is a catch in all this, of course. The barber may say to me, "You cut your kids' hair and I'll educate my kids. Then we'll both be out of a job." In all our striving for independence we may ignore an even more important fact: our interdependence. It is well to face the truth: our complex life makes it impossible for us to do things ourselves except in very limited areas. When I take my car to the garage for repairs, I am deeply thankful that there are people and gadgets to help me. I shudder to think of the sort of life I would lead without the butcher, the baker, and the candlestick maker—at least the first two. It is a spiritual feat to stand alone and to defy injustice. But it is also a spiritual victory to realize how much we need one another. I should like to recommend that insight to the barbers' union and to myself.

The Moving Finger Writes

Not the Picture Tube

We've just had our TV fixed. Fortunately it was a minor operation and there was no malignancy. We did not have to replace the picture tube. For $18.71 we have been restored to normalcy. The neighborhood had begun to demand it. Too many casual visits were developing around suppertime. There was always an Olsson around with the vacant stare and the half-open mouth. Now the family is complete again. I am surprised how little has changed during our Rip van Winkle absence. They are still showing the same movie from the Battle of the Midway. On "What's My Line?" John Daly looks a little older and Arlene Francis has had a hair rinse, but they are using the same old blindfolds and the same gags. Last night was Old Home Week on "What's My Line?" They had invited back the girdle salesman and the lady wrestler for the 37th time.

The Evil Eye

Looking at TV momentarily has revived my old gripe. We are becoming a nation of starers. The camera film has enabled us to capture and to freeze and hence to store segments of past time and of distant places. The tape recorder has done the same for the spoken word. It has become a curious mania to have pictures and tapes of everything. You cannot attend a public function which is not intruded upon by popping flash bulbs. No rite, no sanctity, no private feeling is immune from this intrusion. I have seen flash bulbers hanging from balconies and I have seen them creeping on hands and knees down church aisles and I have been interrupted in the midst of a burst of oratory by the wink of their evil eye. It used to be that we would see the bride after she was properly dressed, veiled, and married. Now we see her from the moment that she arises on the day of her nuptials: bobby pins, pincurlers, yawns, breakfast toast, and kiss from papa, until she disappears in the hotel elevator. And we get everything in between: the over-dressed relatives, the four toasters and the sixteen casseroles, the bridegroom slipping on his cuff links, and the minister struggling into his robe. The shy kiss of the bride, the prayer of the pastor, the tears of the bride's mother (who will now have to do her own dishes), and the smile of the father (who can now adjust his annuities)—all this is open to the cold stare of the camera's eye and is preserved for posterity.

And what shall we say of tapes of sermons and conferences and family gatherings which all our piety and all our wit cannot erase?

The Waters of
Lethe

Are we so sure that everything must live on? Isn't it a great blessing that some things pass away? Augustine thanks God because he in his great mercy causes things to pass away, "for they had no way to pass away, unless thou upheldest them." The Greeks believed that the waters of Lethe caused forgetfulness. Our fathers used to say about our sins, "When God forgives, he forgets." We are thankful that last summer's leaves are already on their way to become next year's soil. Why should we be so hesitant to forget not only life's sorrows but even some of its joys? The Christian doctrine of the resurrection does not emphasize the conservation of everything. Then it would enjoin mummifying the body. It emphasizes glorification, that is, God's recreative work. Not, we shall be preserved, but *we shall be changed*. We shall be what we are but also what grace can make us.

The Work of the
Imagination

From one point of view all the recording we are doing blocks the resurrective and recreative power of the imagination. Should we remember through our memories and imaginations or through snapshot and tape recording? That depends upon what we are remembering and for what purpose. The historian had better trust the tape and the film. But the poet had better use his memory and his imagination. Wordsworth writes about his lyrical poems:

> The principle object . . . was to choose incidents
> and situations from common life . . . and at the
> same time to throw over them a certain coloring of
> imagination whereby ordinary things should be
> presented to the mind in an unusual aspect . . .

Such remembering has given us such incomparable poems
as "I wandered lonely as a cloud" in which Wordsworth
tells us that he really did not *see* the daffodils until long
after he had seen them:

> *For oft when on my couch I lie*
> *In vacant or in pensive mood*
> *They flash upon that inward eye*
> *Which is the bliss of solitude.*

Like poets, brides and bridegrooms had better throw over
their past the "coloring of imagination." To look at old
snapshots is an invitation to hilarity. The camera lied. We
never looked like that. What we were really like is more
finely etched on the film of the inward eye and graved upon
the delicate surface of the inward ear.

Robin Hood and His Merry In-laws

Saturday Night in Somonauk

I have just been arrested. I have hence felt my kinship with galley slaves and the wretches of Dostoevsky's "underground." Now Bunyan is my brother and so is the Count of Monte Cristo. The only rub is that it had to happen in Somonauk. To fall foul of the law in Baghdad or Omsk is digestible, but to be arrested in Somonauk, Illinois, is to drink bitterness to the dregs. It was at dusk a Saturday evening in mid-November. I knifed through the gloom of the Illinois prairie unaware that I had entered, traversed, and passed beyond Somonauk. Suddenly the murk was pierced by a glaring light, and I looked back to see a police car lit up like a pinball machine. With icy calm I flipped open my wallet and waited, but I knew from the sinister quality of the air that I had had it.

The Majesty of
the Law

I was invited to inspect the newly-purchased speed clock on the squad car which announced that I had headed through the fields of Somonauk at 43 miles per hour. Before such incontrovertible scientific certitude my bravado melted. I was invited to return to the City Hall to await the Majesty of the Bench. City Hall was wrapped in gloom, but there were keys, and I was brought into the inner sanctum over creaking floors. I was permitted to sit by the roll-top desk which constituted the High Tribunal. The arresting officer called a number, there was a childish shriek at the other end; I could see the Bench surrounded by his happy little family and waiting for the Gene Autry show on TV. Now he must be called out into the chill to defend the bastions of the Law.

While we waited for the Bench to appear, the arresting officer tried to be sociable. He preached a little sermon on the evils of Speed; he recounted how just last week he had been arrested in Chicago for transgressing the speed limit by 3 miles; he mourned that his star and his credentials meant nothing before Chicago justice. I could feel the sweat form around my temples. If I were to constitute some sort of middleman in the vendetta between Somonauk and Chicago, things were going to be rough.

I did not appear to be an animated listener; the arresting officer gave up trying to be a good fellow and began reading a magazine. In a few moments the Bench entered. I stood up out of some obscure need of protocol but was told to sit down. I sat down. The Bench addressed himself to some legal forms: the ticket, a waiver of jury trial, a complaint for the violation of statute, a receipt form. There was no periwig or crimson robe. There was no lighted candle or swearing on the Bible or clanking of chains. There was only a ball point pen moving greasily over forms. After what seemed a long time, the waiver of jury trial was pushed toward me. I began reading the fine print. The Bench looked mildly annoyed. Gene Autry was saddling his horse, and I was being difficult. The bleak prospect of having to return to Somonauk to face a jury of my peers in that hospitable village decided me. I waived trial by jury. After another little homily by the Bench in which I was assured that the Village of Somonauk wished only to be fair, I was fined $18.00 and held for a judgment of $1.00 and court costs of $3.00. Constable fees were waived. I staggered out into the gloom of Somonauk remembering Thomas Gray's lines about the English village:

> *Some mute inglorious Milton here may rest.*
> *Some Cromwell guiltless of his country's blood.*

I wasn't so sure.

Reflections on an
Empty Pocketbook

Two conclusions force themselves on your benumbed consciousness as you head back into the stream of traffic:

1. The medieval character of our American police systems. The village police, the county police, the state police, the FBI, the T men struggle to define areas of

jurisdiction. On the same national highway there may be four or five different speed limits depending upon the caprice of the hamlet fathers.

2. The crudeness of human justice. Like all people freshly deprived of $22.00, I reflected sourly on the degree of my guilt. The Apostle Peter enjoined the infant church to *suffer innocently*. But one wonders if anyone ever suffers without a degree of guilt. Or innocence. The saint receiving his wreath of fragrant amaranth must feel a stab of guilt. The felon hounded down and sniffing the first wisp of potassium cyanide in the gas chamber must feel bewilderment in the face of the gravity of his punishment. The saint must know that he was never quite that good and the felon that he was never quite that bad.

Politics Without Protocol

For Shame!
For Shame!

In Washington recently I went to see the Capitol. I had never visited the higher brain center of my country. We had had a nodding acquaintance, and I felt it was about time to be properly introduced. Millions of people had the same idea at the same time. We drifted around in shambling flocks bellwethered by guides who looked as if they had trouble with their feet. We learned about all the obscure Italian artists, the gold leaf, and the undistinguished statuary. It is impossible to find duller sculpture anywhere outside a Bohemian cemetery. The worst piece had been dragged into the crypt where it shared emptiness with Washington's unoccupied tomb (he is buried at Mount Vernon). It represents four suffragettes emerging from a block of marble. No anti-feminist could ever devise a more mournful fate for these good ladies than did their female sculptor. The thought of all these activistic women imprisoned from the waist down in imperishable stone and put away in the basement while their male antagonists are allowed to orate at will fifty feet above them bedews the face with tears.

Who Is
My Congressman?

After the Cook's tour of the Capitol, I discovered that I must have a door pass in order to enter the galleries of the House or Senate. This pass must be secured from your congressman or your senator. The Senate was not sitting but the House was. I consequently struck out for the House Office Building. On the way I was greeted by a kindly man who looked as if he wanted to be helpful. I gave him the opportunity. Getting a pass, he assured me, was a simple matter. If I would tell him the name of my congressman, he would escort me to the office. I contemplated something vague at the horizon. My congressman? He smiled at me helpfully. Perhaps if I couldn't remember my congressman, I would let him know my congressional district. My district? I acted as if I hadn't heard. He repeated his request. The number of my congressional district in Chicago? My brain spun around like a wheel of fortune. Blank. Pathetically blank. He refused to be discouraged. "I shall mention the Illinois congressmen," he said brightly, "and when you hear the name of your man, stop me." He began reading. I listened. I concentrated so that the veins protruded from my forehead, "Beezie, Begun, Cahill, Cooley, Caxton, Dingley . . ." He was scanning my face. It remained tense and idiotic.

A half-hour later, with the aid of a building guard, a gray-haired gentleman who may have been a congressman, a gracious secretary from California and Devon in Chicago,

and a congressman across the sewage canal from my district, I clutched the coveted green pass in my hand. It
guaranteed that I was, if not an enlightened, at least a harmless citizen.

The House
Beautiful

I had been warned not to expect much in the House. I
hope all the sweet-faced high school children who were
doing Washington had been similarly warned. A Washington columnist once called Congress "the largest organized
monkey house in the world." This is calumny. Most of the
work in Congress is done in committee, and I am quite
sure that most of the men on Capitol Hill are conscientious.
But despite this, the effect on a spectator of an empty and
inattentive chamber is not reassuring. There were not over
thirty men in attendance. This figure includes the eminent
as well as attendants, reporters, pages, etc. The few who
were there looked as interested in what was going on as
the owl train crowd in Union Station at 2.03 a.m.

As the Twig Is Bent

Perhaps this is essential. But I am led to wonder at the
impact of this slovenliness on the growing generation. Can't
the argument which keeps the Senate and the House
manned by a skeleton crew be applied equally well to a high
school classroom? Perhaps the absentees on a spring afternoon are studying in the library or working on experiments
in the lab. Perhaps. But there is always a suspicion that the
absent legislator, like the absent adolescent, is goofing off.
I have a strong conviction that if we are going to bring

young people to Washington in droves to see our government at work, we ought not to show them the slouch and the yawn. Let the merciful curtain of secrecy be drawn over such sanctified boredom. And let America of tomorrow be shown the heroes of the past in pure Carrara marble. They may be dull sculpture, but at least they are present and accounted for.

It Is the Thing to Do

Ode to Duty

Some years ago a streetcar ad for Alka Seltzer carried the following sentiment,

> *On Thanksgiving we give thanks;*
> *It is the thing to do.*

Trivial things may sometimes be profound, and this is an example. For many, if not most, people life is a succession of things which "must be done." We begin early with the duty of keeping clean. There is a sad splendor about the rebellion of a boy against having his neck washed. He will lose. It's written in the stars. He must wash. He must not bolt his food. He must get to bed. He must go to school. He cannot be late. He cannot be absent. He cannot be rude or sassy or flippant. He must respect his elders. He must learn to treat girls with the respect appropriate to their sex. He must master a musical instrument, spelling, grammar, his temper, his voice, his finances, his beard. It is the thing to do. And for the little girl the road is even stonier. After a few brief years she must be well-groomed, courteous, cultured, modulated and at the same time enthusiastic, energetic, and spontaneous. She must be attractive enough to attract boys, but she must do this in the right way and with the right effect. It is the thing to do.

The Phantom
of Delight

It would be "romantic" in the worst sense to ask for something else. Margaret Mead's earlier studies of the Pacific islands, which criticized "westernizing" missionaries for disrupting the idyll of the noble savage, do not impress me. I am not convinced that civilization makes people unhappier; I am quite certain that Christianity rightly interpreted is the hope of the whole world even though I do not believe that an Ubangi Christian needs to brush his teeth with fluoride or wear dacron in order to be a saint. There are certain things which must be done if civilization is not to sink into savagery: boys must wash their necks and learn grammar, and girls must master the complex art of womanhood. But certain things ought *not* to be considered duty. To put them in that category is to destroy them. We ought never to be *forced to enjoy* music or art or literature. We must obviously be introduced to them in the process of our schooling. Boys and girls should be confronted with Bach and Braque and Ben Jonson. But once the introductions are made, a friendship for the arts must develop as naturally as any other friendship. And if acquaintance does not ripen into love, people should not be forced to be *appreciative* because it is the thing to do. To see a grown male, wedged into an opera seat and clutching a concert program, wage a losing battle with his eyelids or to see him plod around an art gallery looking for "compositional unity" and "contrapuntal massifs"—because it is the thing to do—is to witness once more the refined torture of the Inquisition. There is just as much sense in cultural coercion as in rounding up artists and art critics and forcing them to watch the Dodgers because that is the thing to do.

When First It Gleamed

I say all this because, amateur though I am, I like art galleries. And I want other people to like them, if not in the same way, at least for their own good reasons. The other day I saw the National Gallery of Art in Washington for the first time. I had only a couple of hours, but they were hours of pure delight. First of all, because I like color and line without always knowing why, and there is a festival of color from Cimabue to Dali in that vast building. Secondly, because European art before 1500 is devoted to the great motifs of the faith—the birth, life, and passion of our Lord. When you stand before these unending variations of the cross of Christ and see the love which burns in the color, you enter a new dimension. People do not paint like this or adore like this because "it is the thing to do." The adoration and the art are the fruit of an unforced act of attention which Bernard of Clairvaux calls *diligence*. It has nothing to do with duty in the ordinary sense. It is the preoccupation of love. It is in this spirit we ought to worship, and marry, and listen to music, and serve our neighbor and perhaps take down our storm windows.

Down You Go

Whatsoever Things Are True

On state occasions Northwestern University undergraduates sing as their Alma Mater the moving climax of Paul's letter to the Philippians. The melody is "St. Antoni Chorale," immortalized in Brahms' "Variations on a Theme by Haydn." But if the grapevine is correct, Northwestern students do not turn for truth in the direction the aspostle would have proposed. For "whatsoever is true" they depend on TV celebrity Bergen Evans, whose witticisms still enthrall eggheads and confound the simple.

Milk Shake Mythology

Campus talk has it that in the university huddles where clear-eyed students mix malts with misanthrophy and take their first heady nip of Jean Paul Sartre, heads turn and a liturgical silence falls when Bergen Evans makes an appearance. His classes in literature are crowded with those

with and without wedding garments; many come unbidden
to the feast. The kernels of truth which fall from his lips
are snatched up eagerly by his followers and are then
ground and baked into a sacramental cake which nourishes
the novices in the faith. One of these kernels (which may
be halfway myth) is a reputed statement that no intelligent
person within the last hundred years has believed in God.
Another: that Jesus may never have existed.

Ingersoll
Redivivus

I don't know when Mr. Evans last refreshed his notes, but
if these statements are correct, their inspiration must come
from the 1920s, when Bergen was an undergraduate in
wild attack on the Presbyterian prejudices of his ancestors.
It is inconceivable that anyone who has followed the course
of Western thought with sensitivity during the past thirty
years could make such statements. They are fusty as the
rhetoric of Robert Ingersoll. They reflect not a soberly
skeptical mind or even the majesty of classical atheism but
the be-pimpled pose of Rakitin in Dostoevski's *Brothers
Karamazov:* "a young man bent on a career." In an America dedicated to shallow faith such posing may prove profit-
able among the young and the bewildered. But it is inconceivable how it can impress those who have taken a second
course in introduction to philosophy.

Humble Pie
A la Mode

Beneath Mr. Evans' unbitter cynicism there is a nine-
teenth-century faith in human reason and human creativity.

67

It is the faith of some benign philanthropists who endow dog hospitals and public birdbaths and of kindly dowagers who have substituted public lectures for prayer meetings. The recent Freud centennial affirmed its belief in what men can do for themselves if they will only try a little harder and have a little more faith. The world wars (I and II) had shaken this faith, it was admitted, but there was no reason to believe that these wars manifested any permanent darkness in human nature. The sun of reason was now rising with healing in its wings.

Coupled with this optimism is a new and strange kind of humility. It is a humility which says, "Man is only nature; let him be content with what he is." It has always seemed curious to me that if man is only nature he should have to be exhorted to be natural. We don't have to tell a turnip or a gnu to stop having immortal yearnings. A turnip is most solidly turnipish whatever we say. And a gnu remains most gnu-like even though we bring him into an art gallery.

Emperor Worm

But a man is never just one thing. He is not just an animal. Or just a spirit. Or an angel. Or a god. A man is a man because he is a composite of many contradictions. Pascal was right when he spoke of man as having the sublimity of a judge and the lowliness of a worm. Consequently if man insists upon emphasizing only his worminess in order that he may rule the world as "Emperor Worm," he is not humble at all but arrogant and rude. This is the sort of false humility which breathes in the proud words of Cosimo de Medici when he says about the Christian faith, "I will not strive so high nor fall so low." It is not Cosimo's decision or Bergen Evans' decision. We are what we are: God's creatures who through some primal indignity have handed ourselves over to the world, the flesh, and the devil. Every proud word which tries to deny our estate merely enunciates it the more. We are rebels who unless we capitulate to our most merciful Lord become increasingly thin and sour. Such acidulous thinness is the climate of hell. It issues out not in hisses, as Milton maintains, but in a whine—the Whine Everlasting.

Forgiveness

The Red Face

Few things embarrass me as much as being asked for
forgiveness. Before proceeding, let me say that I am not
arguing against my duty to forgive. This is clearly enjoined
in the Gospel. We are to love and to forgive people even
when they are nasty to us. I have all that fairly straight.
What bothers me is the process whereby forgiveness is
sought and granted. Someone comes to me and says,
"Brother, I have had some unkind thoughts about you. I
can't sleep. Will you forgive me?"

Heartburn

I wonder, for example, about motives. Why do we seek
someone's forgiveness? Is it because we have hurt our
brother and now out of love for him we want to heal his
hurt? Or is it because in hurting him we have injured ourselves? Our malice is causing us heartburn or fluttering
eyelids or a crawling scalp. And so we go to the brother
and say, "I did you an injury, and it has upset my psychoso-

70

matic balance. You must forgive me." Or we have a bad conscience, not because we have caused pain to our brother but because causing pain is naughty and must be taken care of before we can feel the smile of approval upon us. And so we ask for forgiveness.

There is some merit, of course, in doing penance because we are afraid of the consequences of an act. A lot of goodness in the world is inspired by fear of the effects of badness; ulcers, loss of status, and Hell are deterrents of evil which must be reckoned with. But this is an inferior kind of penitence. Thomas Aquinas calls it *attrition* and distinguishes it from *contrition*, which is genuine sorrow for sin. Soul winning, for example, is in the category of attrition when it is inspired by a sort of profit motive. I try to win a soul not because I love the soul and want to see it saved but because I love myself and want to be approved. In God's economy that sort of bargaining no doubt has its place, but it is well to understand the motive.

The Questionable
Scruple

There is, nevertheless, another reason why I am shy about being asked for forgiveness. I am sure that a lot of people are overly scrupulous about their sins toward me. Have they hurt me as deeply as they think? In the Christian church we have had so much talk about the evil of gossip that we have guilt complexes about disliking people and expressing that dislike. But it is a transparent fact that people do annoy us. This is not entirely a matter of malice. It may be a matter of temperament. Some people bother us because of the way they manage their eyebrows or answer the telephone or break into conversations; others because they are fussy-fussy about nickels and dimes; others because they are sloppy and miss appointments or leave Kleenex around; still others because they are milkily meek.

Is it my Christian duty to belie these qualities in a burst of amiable hypocrisy? And must my mouth be sealed forever against expressing my feelings? I don't believe it. I accord my brethren the right to dislike me for one of a number of reasons and the right to articulate their dislike. For this they do not need to ask my forgiveness. The childish epigram still holds:

> *Sticks and stones may break my bones,*
> *But names will never hurt me.*

Furthermore, if they feel the urge, they may tell me about my weaknesses. I won't like it, but I'll grit my teeth and hang on.

The Right to Dislike

What we have a right to ask of Christian brethren is honesty and the sort of forgiving love which is the gift of grace. An honest aversion based upon first-hand acquaintance is one thing. Blind prejudice is something else again. But after they know us, people ought to have the right to dislike us. Nevertheless, if they are Christians, in the midst of their annoyance they have the obligation to love us, not, mind you, because we are lovable, but simply because it is commanded. This means, first of all, praying for our salvation. It also means forgiving us. Much, much more than being asked for forgiveness we need to be forgiven.

Grass

The Grass Withers

The time is now fast approaching when we shall know if it was worth doing. I mean digging up the lawn again. And trying to follow all the advice tossed over the picket fence by the well-meaning. There is the gaunt bony man of great age who tugs his thatch of beard and mumbles, "bone meal." There is the lady from the garden club who suggests "creeping bent." There are the advocates of sheep manure, black dirt, peat moss, mulch, compost, rye, fescue, blue grass, and clover. There are the apostles of sunshine who tell us to cut down our ancient elms and hackberries. And there are the pessimists who shake their heads and talk about the chemicals in the air and in the Chicago water system.

Grass and
Greed

Once upon a time we had a neighbor who wanted to sell his bungalow. From the windows of his house, where he sat waiting like a genial spider, he could see the sterile patch of cracked clay which forms our front lawn. He was afraid that his asking price for the bungalow would shrink unless something could be done about our grass. It is comforting to have your neighbors worry about your lot. One August afternoon he came timidly and offered to buy black dirt and lawn seed to improve our grass. And his profit. We bore the insult with compressed lips.

The Tender
Shoot

For years we had bought leaf mould, cow droppings, and synthetic chemicals pink as the pillars of Karnak. We had considered importing a wise man from Vermont who whispers to the grass when the moon is thin. Our coaxing labors had been rewarded with a few fragile shoots. In May and June, that is. The little platoon of blades had formed a focus for our happy kith. "You are getting grass," they would say with the enthusiasm of an ancient Jew announcing his paternity or an Oklahoma petroleum engineer reporting a gusher. But nothing came of it. In July there was a subtle change. Deepening shadows under the eyes. A transparency of the flesh. And in August the last little yellow blade donned its funereal robes and was gathered to its fathers.

A Reproach and
a Hissing

This was hard to bear. At night we could hear people pass by on the sidewalk. Their heels made a different sound when they hit our cracked concrete. A hollow sound. Then the words would float up and in through the screens: "Must

74

be Okies living here now. . . . Used to be a nice place when the Swedes owned it. . . . You'd think they'd do something to get a little grass . . ." And so forth. In the darkness we held fists to our mouths to muffle the sobs.

The Valley of Avilion

Now I understand that there is something new. A hardy type of Korean grass developed by the U.S. Department of Agriculture. It grows in cinders and gravel and even in Chicago clay. It doesn't need fertilizing, watering, or mowing. In the winter it shines with the luster of pure gold. In the summer it is richly green like Scandinavian envy. It is a sort of living toupee. (In passing I should like to stress that we do not offer any item mentioned in this column for sale. There has been one inquiry from a court house in New Mexico about the pigeon patent.) When I heard about this Korean grass I had a lovely vision. It is August under the umbrageous verdure of the elms and hackberries, a green springy carpet of the lushest grass. Unfenced and unguarded it forms the romping place for the neighborhood's twenty-three children, forty-six dogs, bicycles, perambulators, and golf enthusiasts. The lawn mower and the hose gather dust in the tool shed. I lie stretched out in a canvas chair watching my community at play in a new Eden. A line from Tennyson whispers itself in my ear:

> . . . the island-valley of Avilion,
> Where falls not hail, or rain, or any snow,
> Nor ever wind blows loudly; but it lies
> Deep-meadowed, happy, fair with orchard lawns
> And bowery hollows. . . .

On Second Thought

But on second thought I shall not buy any Korean grass. It's too easy. It's not really any fun. It's like a Mohammedan heaven. Now that the possibility of getting away from spading, and weeding, and sowing in tears is upon us, I don't want it. Whatever the verdure of the Christian heaven is, I am sure it is not Korean grass. The leaves of the trees are for the healing of the nations and such vegetation grows out of suffering love. The river of the water of life which is bright as crystal was once the color of blood. That is why it can nourish the tree of real everlastingness.

I Got a Robe

The Robes of Justice

A hot-weather topic in the Chicago papers currently is the practice of wearing judicial robes in court. Some people feel that it is not democratic to wear anything which sets you apart from the populace. Others feel that a robe is a violation of Christian principle since it is a badge of carnal pride. Others again dismiss the robe in typical American fashion as being inefficient and uncomfortable. I feel particularly sensitive on the subject because I have just suffered through three academic processions in which I wore an academic gown.

Solons in Sport Shirts

No one could possibly argue that these habiliments are either efficient or comfortable. I should not feel easy about answering a 4-11 alarm or rescuing a drowning swimmer in my academic gown. On a recent occasion I suffered the acute embarrassment of having my hood (a kind of colorful cloth yoke originally used to hold the books and apples of Oxford undergraduates) slip down over my knees in a moment of high dignity. Nothing has amused my friends and foes more than this little *faux pas;* I looked, they say, like a hobbled circus horse attempting a pirouette. How much happier life would be if academic processions, courts of high justice, and dinners of state could be lived through in sport shirts or T shirts. The various academic grades could be designated by color; baby blue for Bachelors; robust red for Masters; mouse gray for Doctors.

All God's Chillun Got Robes

"No," say my democratic friends, "you miss the point. Any discrimination is undemocratic. By wearing distinctive dress you induce feelings of inferiority in the masses. Either everyone should have a robe or no one should have a robe. Designations of rank are feudal, fascistic, and discriminatory. They are a soil for special privilege."

Many years ago Thomas Carlyle wrote a book called *Sartor Resartus* (the tailor reclothed). In it he developed the thesis that "Society . . . is founded upon cloth." Without clothes, says Carlyle, the whole fabric of society would dissolve. This is a thought to be pondered. In swimming trunks the most ponderous pontiff seems no more impressive than his chauffeur. Carlyle visualizes the catastrophic effect of having "a naked Duke of Windlestraw addressing a naked House of Lords."

By clothes Carlyle does not mean merely cloth and fur but the symbols in which we are clothed. The bus driver, the policeman, the fireman, the custodian of a building, the craftsman at his job, all the professions, the father as father and the mother as mother, even the child in the family—all of these are invested with symbols of status, more or less inviolable.

And yet beneath all these symbols, beneath the clothes, people are people, sharing alike in their nakedness the dignity and the shame, the exaltation and the weakness of mankind.

A Multitude . . .
In White Robes

The Christian faith is even more radically leveling. It insists that before God men are not only men but sinners and that if they are to be clothed at all it must be in the white robes of an imputed righteousness. Hence the early Christian practice of wearing only white and the development gradually of monastic dress: uniform, coarse, unadorned.

Democracy or
Anarchy?

What should be our attitude as Americans and Christians toward rank and its symbols? Shall we ignore distinctions and shall we clothe everyone in the same good gray cloth? Well, in the first place, to ignore differences is probably to falsify the nature of existence, at least to falsify history. There are differences in responsibility, in acumen, in power. The parent is not the child. The teacher is not the student. The doctor is not the patient.

In the second place, it is probably necessary to symbolize,

however simply, all legitimate differences. The President of the United States may not wear a crown or a toga, but he is invested with symbols of his office. The story is told of how Calvin Coolidge dressed down an impertinent boy at Superior High School for some flippant remark to him. Sooner or later parents, teachers, and pastors must similarly assume the vesture of office. It is well that when they do, they do so reluctantly and with a touch of wry humor, remembering that under the robes they too are "a forked radish with a head fantastically carved."

Fate

Whatever Will Be Will Be

A ditty is being sung currently of a folksy Italian origin. Two lines go: "Whatever will be will be, the future's not ours to see." This sounds godly enough. I am sure that the average American, if he thinks at all about these things, feels that this comes close to the Christian Gospel. Here you have the rule of providence and man's inability to penetrate its mystery. The song is given an additional touch of orthodoxy by the fact that its homely philosophy is sung by a mother to her children. You can see the tender-eyed Italian mama surrounded by her inquisitive brood. You can see her shrug her adequate shoulders when the kids ask if they will be rich. "Who knows," she says, "who knows? All this is fate. Someone or something is calling the plays. Whatever will be will be. *Che sara, sara.*"

Your Number
Comes Up

I once had a very able professor who belonged to the turn-of-the-century skeptics. He was not an imaginative atheist. Most of the time I found his fulminations against the faith more dull than dangerous. But one day he got warmed up on "fate." His theory was that Christians, Moslems, Jainists, Aztecs, Hairy Ainus, Kaffirs, Kalmuks, and Kanakas, whatever their theologies, had only one religion —a blind belief in the wheel of fate. He spoke of a subterranean, dark, and desperate trust in the machinery of existence, which really governs our actions much more than rational creeds. Christians too, he leered, will talk about their "lucky days"; they will refer to their "number coming up"; they will talk about a bullet or a shell which missed them as not carrying "their number." He was most convincing and most disturbing.

The Numbered
Grenade

I thought of this discussion some years later. We were maneuvering in the Mojave Desert, than which the American continent has nothing more achingly void and lonely. One night as we bent over our dismal B ration—dehydrated carrots, dehydrated potatoes, dehydrated beef—and let our vision sweep over the dehydrated sand which whispered around us, the conversation turned to a dashing cavalry captain who that day had been demonstrating home-made grenades. Something went wrong with the demonstration and the captain was terribly mangled. He never recovered consciousness. "Well," said someone, "I guess his number was up." "Yup," said someone else, "when it's your turn, you gotta go." They turned to me for theological support. They would be facing the same sort of peril themselves in a few days or weeks. They wanted to play percentages. They wanted to believe that they might be lucky gamblers and come up holding the right card or the right number on the dice.

The Father of
Mercies

I wanted to tell them that life isn't like that. At least God is not like that. He is not Thomas Hardy's idiotic somnambulist who picks the fated number out of his hat. He is the Father of mercies and the God of all comfort. Which means that with him nothing happens from impulse. What happens is related to his wisdom and his charity. This does not make life turned, polished, and smooth. Life even for a Christian, perhaps particularly for a Christian, is coarse-textured. The best people have had to suffer cruelly, not only at the hands of other men but from the savagery of nature. I think of missionaries ravaged by disease, struck by lightning, stung by venomous snakes. "Of whom the world was not worthy." They were brought to revise any unreal estimate of their existence. The light blue nursery walls were blown away. They found themselves in the austerity of flint and naked light. The place of the skull. Nevertheless, and this is the heart of the matter, they did not feel *out of relationship*. They did not think of themselves as IBM cards waiting for a cold key. Their election proceeded from a heart, inscrutable perhaps, but con-

cerned. Even the most terrible cry of all, the word of
dereliction from the cross, is directed to God as person.

The Unshrugging
Shoulders

Christians, consequently, do not shrug their shoulders
about the future. They do not make the future all by themselves of course. But they are not outside of it. What will
be will be because they and the Holy Ghost decide.

Mama

Pastels and Polka Dots

I saw my first polka dotted hard-top the other day. Any time now the cars will come with detachable plastic ruffles. And decals. The interiors are beginning to look like expensive French boudoirs in the style of Louis XIV. "We called in the ladies," say the car manufacturers. The male protest is the European sports car and, in the lowlier brackets, two carburetors and two exhaust pipes: roughness, noise, smell, peeling tires. But the Jaguars, the MG's, and even the Volkswagens are waging a losing battle against the woman behind the steering wheel. Soon the two exhaust pipes will be exuding perfumed concertos and the wild-eyed kid in the careening fire-wagon will be domesticated. The future belongs to mama.

The Hand That Rocks the Cradle

It was not always thus. The frenzy for feminism in the nineteenth century came as a legitimate protest against a world dominated by men. An industrial society created social needs and the leisure to worry about them, especially among women of the middle classes. Hence we get the suffragette, the Lady Bountiful, the temperance advocate, the anti-vivisectionist, the utopian, the institutionalist. We get Carry Amelia Nation, Frances E. Willard, Clarissa Harlowe Barton—women with steel nibs in their eyes and ink in their veins. We get Florence Nightingale and Margaret Fuller. We get women who want so much to be recognized as women that they take the name George: George Eliot and George Sand. And we get institutions. There are homes for everything: orphans, soldiers' widows, unwed mothers, fallen women, escaped slaves, exhausted dray horses, deserted pets. We get lectures. The potted palms, the water carafe, the yellow oak lectern, and the vivid charts become the setting for the harangue, "Organize!" "Demand a vote!" "Attack!" "Don't shoot till you see the whites of their eyes!"

Rocks the Boat

The real villain in this piece was not so much the blubbery beer baron or the toss pot as the Male. The male dominated everything except the nursery. He was a pompous pouter pigeon with stiff shirt front, brushed sideburns, fat gold watch chain, thick eyebrows, and beefy oratory. Everything seems to have provided an opportunity for a major address. The mustache was wiped with a cambric handkerchief, the majestic throat was cleared, and father delivered his opinion with the protocol of a Supreme Court verdict.

Small wonder that women began to shoot their little shafts into the stuffed shirt. Francis Willard wrote, "The many make the household but only *one* the home." The "*one*" homemaker was, of course, mama. Women quoted Abraham Lincoln's words, "All that I am and all I ever hope to be I owe to my angel mother," and nodded their bonneted heads. And so the avalanche started. "What is home without a mother?" "The hand that rocks the cradle rules the world," etc. Silk sofa pillows, ceramic plaques, and framed mottoes began to speak from every home in the Union their gospel of womanhood and motherhood. *Daughters* of the American Revolution, The *Women's* Christian Temperance Union—the feminine is kept in the foreground.

Her Mother and I Do

The retreat of the Prince Albert became a rout. The beards disappeared. Then the mustaches. The starched collars wilted. Grown men began to wear the clothes of little boys. Knickers. Knee-length pants. Sport shirts open at the throat. The watch strapped to the wrist. And mama, confronted no longer by the austerely masculine, began in some instances to think of papa as a boy. Boys need to be told what to do, and papa was told. Even in that high moment of his familial sovereignty—the giving of his daughter in marriage—he was now directed to alter the tradition of the centuries and to confess meekly that he was no longer able to do this himself. Mama had to help. When the preacher asked, "Who giveth this woman to be married to this man?" papa said, "Her mother and I do."

The Lords of Creation

The worm has turned. But it is well to remember that woman is no more suited to the mantle of divinity than man. It was the mother of the race who was tempted to "become a god." Womanhood, even motherhood, is not above sinful corruption. The "will to power" may mask itself behind protestations of love; children may be forced to remain children into adulthood because mama does not want to relinquish her authority.

Man has been dethroned as the "lord of creation," thanks to Susan Brownell Anthony and *Parents Magazine*. But who can cope with mama?

Separate Vacations

Those Friends Thou Hast, Grapple Them

Some years ago one of the spinsters who write advice on marriage suggested that husband and wife take separate vacations as a device to bolster sagging romance. The theory was that after spending three weeks on the beach at Ocean City, hubby would come racing back starry-eyed to his wife returning from her holiday with the children on the family farm in Kansas. Familiarity breeds contempt. Absence makes the heart grow fonder. The theory was that this separation would cause the shy violets of married love to bud once more.

I am not prepared to offer any rebuttal of this theory. I should nevertheless like to contribute a concept of separate vacations in another realm.

It happens now and then when close friends gather around a smoking cup of coffee that if the hour is late and reason is befuddled, someone will propose a shared vacation. "Why don't you go with us to Crow Lake this year? The cabin has four bedrooms and we'll share expenses." All sorts of reasons present themselves: the birched beauties of Crow Lake, the flow of moonlight across the water, the roaring fire in the rude stone fireplace on cool nights (and at Crow the nights are always cool), the opportunity to finish that interesting conversation on inhabited planets which never gets wound up in the city, the chance to explore that intriguing bit of autobiography which requires a more intimate setting, the possibility of a Scrabble marathon. Before anyone knows what has happened the dark plot has been hatched.

Confusion at Crow Lake

It is all a mistake, of course. To go as guests to Crow Lake is one thing. To go there as partners in a sylvan utopia is quite another. There is a universally accepted host-guest protocol. The host must be generous, inventive, indulgent. The guest must be grateful, cooperative, and cautious. For example, if the host serves sweetbreads, tripe, chicken livers, or raw oysters, the guest must seem to enjoy it. If the guest's children kick up the gladioli beds, tease the dog to madness, break a Sevres vase, or ridicule the menu, the host must smile and respond in one of a half dozen bromides fashioned just for hosts, such as, "Boys will be boys," "We were all young once," "Nobody cares about that old vase anyway," or "I like children to have spirit!" This is understood and accepted.

But there is no protocol for a shared vacation. Friends trying to live together as a family are neither fish nor fowl. The relationship is too intimate for friends. You should not see your friend as a friend for twenty-four hours a day. If he were your guest or your host, you would both be wearing the fig leaves of the fiction which keeps life orderly. But in a shared vacation all is revealed. You discover that your friends are hopelessly sloppy, unpunctual, and thoughtless about the art of living. They discover you to be irritatingly methodical and lacking in humor and grace. There are differences about the quality and quantity of the menu. They eat cereal for breakfast; you break your fast with eggs. They eat butter; you margarine. You don't use the same grace. You pass the food clockwise around the table and hubby serves. They help themselves in a complicated fashion which may work for them but which reduces you to despairing hunger while the dishes pass and repass your nose. Then there are the children. It is a known fact that there are no children so charming as your own. Particularly when you contrast them with the children of your friends. Hence it is quite unreasonable that your friends should want to take their disorderly brood along on a fishing expedition which would be perfectly lovely if the only children were your Oswald and Cynthia. The final scene in this dismal drama is a pair of fiercely whispered conversations behind the knotty pine doors of Leisure Lodge at Crow Lake. "Whose idea was this vacation anyway? I can't stand another minute of it. It must have been your idea. You're always thinking up the bright ones. Why, those people are————."

There is divine sanity in the singleness of the household. Family life belongs to the family. It should not be shared promiscuously with everybody under the illusion that blood and water are the same thing. The home should be open, of course. Christian hospitality is a gift and a virtue. But friends are not kinfolk. To imagine that they are is to violate both the canons of family and of friendship.

Look Homeward, Angel!

The Familiar and
the Strange

Lately in more sophisticated theological circles there has been much talk about the *otherness* of God. Not only is God no longer considered an amiable grandfather; he is talked about as *totaliter aliter,* the wholly other. It is theologically out of fashion to talk about God as having personal attributes; he is something beyond everything but he is not even something, for he is no thing. Between God and us there is an infinite gulf of difference. Every new view is in some sense a corrective of other views. An emphasis upon God's awesome otherness is an important swing of the pendulum away from the "chummified" view of divinity. The Bible sets us right on this point. God is high and lifted up; even the God and Father of Jesus as he is revealed to us in the Gospels has austerity and reserve; he lives within a mystery which may be unfolded but is never exhausted.

Nevertheless, the Bible is *right* in this respect also that it never gives us a depersonalized strangeness. God is not unapproachable. It is a terrible thing to fall into the hands of the living God, but it is also a most merciful thing. At Sinai it is the terror of the Lord which saves Israel from the nameless horror which surrounds her. To know God is to enter into holiness so holy as to shock us into numbness; it is also a homecoming—the savoring of a familiarity so close to us that we break into ecstatic speech.

You Can't Go Home Again

In thinking about God and our destiny as men, it is well to remember this doubleness. Heaven is not just the old familiar places raised to their nth power. There are whimsies along this line. Selma Lagerlöf tells the story of a peasant who did not feel at home in heaven until he found his little croft: the gray house set down in stony fields, the fringe of birches, and the dark woods beyond. And Nathan Söderblom has a moving description of a beggar who is not happy among the many mansions until he is shown an unpretentious house in a remote corner of the heavenly estate. I'll accept this as whimsy and as stating a partial truth; I'll not buy it as doctrinally correct.

Some years ago I went back to the house where I spent four years of my early life. The village was largely unchanged and the house was the same as I remembered it. I had been warned that everything would seem smaller after 30 years. It was not. It was the same. The same color, the same smell, the same relationship of lines. If I could have shrunk to a nine-year-old boy with bare feet and hungry eyes and a stomach which argued unceasingly for its right to be stuffed, there would have been no difference. Now everything was different. I heard of one returning immigrant who asked for the privilege of spending a night in the home he had left fifty years before. I heard of another who because he was rich brought the old family place from Sweden to America and set it up on his estate. But you can't go home again.

Last spring I went back to Sharon, Pennsylvania, where we came as a family direct from Sweden. I had not seen it for twenty-five years. I remembered everything: the brick streets, the old Lafayette School in buff brick, disproportionately high and narrow with the shabby dignity of a penniless *grande dame;* Sheaffer's Grocery Store where I put fifteen pounds of potatoes in brown sacks and plucked innumerable chickens. The smell of fresh blood, steaming wet feathers, rotten potatoes, spilled vinegar, and the general mustiness of the cellar—all came back in a rush. But it was no good. I felt like an old actor revisiting the scene of his labors. The scenery was there but the stage was empty and so were the seats. You can ask time to turn backward, but it won't happen.

God, Who Is Our Home

Thomas Wolfe, who has given me these phrases, was right, of course. There is no return. You can't go home again. And even if you could, you wouldn't want to. But there is a homecoming of much larger significance. God has prepared a better place, says the Book of Hebrews. The Prodigal Son came home to a joy he never knew. Christ found a place better than Nazareth on the other side of the cross. The old and familiar will share in the resurrection but it too must die and "suffer a sea change into something rich and strange."

There Was an Old Woman...

Who Swallowed
a Fly

I am a confirmed believer in the wisdom of Mother
Goose. I don't always understand what the rhymes mean,
but when I do, I am frequently helped by them. Jack
Sprat, for example, says more about marriage than the
Institute for Family Living. And Little Bo Peep is a com-
mentary on the mysterious operations of nature and providence. For this reason I am always happy when a new
nonsense rhyme with the Mother Goose sauciness appears.
The old woman who swallowed a fly is an instance.

This woman who progressively swallows a fly, a spider,
a bird, a cat, a dog, a goat, a cow, and, with tragic finality,
a horse, is not just an eccentric. She is a symbol of the
madness with which we were all afflicted outside the circle
of grace.

I Don't Know Why

The rhyme begins in mystery. It affirms that no one knows why the old woman did what she did, namely, swallow a fly. Perhaps it was accident. Perhaps it was the result of sinful scheming. Perhaps it was the breaking out of repressed impulses. In any event, she performed the deed. And true to the tradition of tragedy, the poem gives us at its very beginning a feeling of gloomy foreboding, "perhaps she'll die."

What concerns me in this little meditation, however, is not so much what finally happens to the old woman ("she's dead, of course") as what might be called the progression of her tragedy, the dark unfoldment of her fate.

For having swallowed the fly, the old woman proceeds to a new folly: she swallows a spider to catch the fly, and then she has to swallow a bird to deal with the spider and so on all the way up to the staggering finale—the last enveloping envelope of the squirming menagerie within her —a living horse: hoof, mane, tail and all.

The drama ends with the solemnity of a tolling bell: *There was an old woman who swallowed a horse. She's dead, of course.*

The Swiss Navy

There is currently a great vogue in America: yachting or, more modestly, boating. Many people living in apartments miles from the water are buying an assortment of craft. These pretty little toys are moored in the various yacht harbors around Chicago. On good week ends, that is, week ends when there is some wind but not too much, the navy puts out to sea. It is a nice sight to see the brave-ly canvassed cat boat or yawl head seaward with mayhap a bronzed youth clinging to the mainmast and his equally bronzed wife stretched out on the decking in togs from Bonwit Teller. But the dear people have swallowed a fly which will presently require the downing of a spider. Be-fore long they will be coveting larger boats and they will be paying docking fees and storage fees. And then there will be a baby, or he'll get transferred to Omaha.

Investment at
Crow Lake

Then there is the summer cottage. I have had that dream too. The sun glints through the birches on limpid water. The lake bottom is the whitest sand. There is the shouting of children. On the carefully groomed lawn which slopes up from the beach to our cottage is a group of people holi-day clad. They are drinking coffee and eating freshly baked pastries from the cottage kitchen. No one seems strained or hurried. Everything goes by itself.

All this can be mine for $2,000 down and $50 per month for ten years. That includes the boat. It is a most tempting offer—a most manageable fly. I almost swallowed it. But I begin to think of all that must follow: another set of storm windows, more paint, more grass seed, more furniture, more payments. Outboard motors for the larger boats and larger boats for the larger motors. More insurance, taxes, fees. And above all more worries. The long nights under the stars at Crow Lake turning on the mattress which was too lumpy for Chicago and saying, "Let's see now, if I pay this bill this month, maybe next month . . ."

Thanks, old woman, for swallowing the horse!

Small Expectations

Breakfast Grumbles

A letter from a young wife with a husband dying of cancer gives me the thought for the week. She writes: "The more severe our trials, the smaller our expectations have grown. Now we are praying merely for the chance to be together a little longer." Letters like this have a way of reaching us on our smallest days. This was the day we grumbled about the consistency of the egg yolk, the lack of crispness in the bacon, the neutrality of the coffee. This was the day when our self-pitying brow wrinkled with irritation because the children were noisy and our favorite shirt had a microscopic wrinkle in the collar. This was the day we expected the heavens to weep and the universe to be prostrated with grief because we missed a three-foot putt on the 14th green, had to wait 23 seconds in a traffic snarl, did not get firsts on the morning paper.

98

Vale of Whimpers

If it is true that our expectations diminish as our trials increase, it is equally true that our demands grow in direct proportion to our blessings. It is easy to recognize the spoiled child: the pouting mouth smeared with his latest sugared bribe, the mistrustful eye, the arrogant demeanor, the insufferable thanklessness. "Spoiled rotten," we say, and shake our sage knobs. "The parents ought to do something about that little menace." True, alas, too true! But who, pray, is going to do something about the bratty adult who has equally unreasonable demands upon existence? What courageous soul is going to take you and me out to the woodshed and set us straight?

The Facts of Life

For spoiledness, whether infant or adult, arises from a false view of life. This view is in part the product of our fabulous era. After staring through the lighted window for thousands of years, the little match girl has finally been invited in to share the glories of the playroom. There are 7,000 dolls, 9,000 teddy bears, 683 rocking horses, 11,000 drums, fifes, and trumpets. She has 14 long tons of candy, a shipload of apples and oranges, and a mountain of raisins.

It is also a product of propaganda. We are being told by practically everybody that the golden age is upon us and that in a few years we shall have a 600-billion-dollar annual economy. The reasoning which follows is simple. If the world is so wonderful, why do I still have pimples?

The Vale of
Tears

When I was a child, we used to sing a great deal about heaven. This earth was a vale of tears, a thornhedge, a cross school. Once it had been a garden, but sin had turned it into a desert. But some day things would be better. There would be wonderful things to eat and drink, there would be close-cropped lawns, there would be music and people in very clean clothes. And there would be a great shining river.

I have not always been sure that the picture of heaven which we were given was accurate. It left out some important features and distorted others. But I am very sure that the view of earthly life was realistic. We have made people believe that earthly existence is a stay at a resort hotel when in fact it is the running of an obstacle course. "The Puritans were right," said a professor of mine who did not make any profession of faith. "They said that life was thorny and hard and it is, it is."

The Tolerable
Reformatory

In *Essays Presented to Charles Williams,* C. S. Lewis writes about his friend:

Charles Williams . . . also said that when young people came to us with their troubles and discontents, the worst thing we could do was tell them that they were not so unhappy as they thought. Our reply ought rather to be, "But of course . . ." For young people usually are unhappy, and the plain

100

truth is often the greatest relief we can give them. The world is painful in any case: but it is quite unbearable if everyone gives us the idea that we are meant to be liking it. Half the trouble is over when that monstrous demand is withdrawn. What is unforgiveable if judged as a hotel may be very tolerable as a reformatory.

To withdraw the "monstrous demand" that all of life should arrange itself prettily around our center is to rediscover how much there is for which we can be effortlessly thankful. The most common capacities: to eat when we are hungry, to work with our hands or our heads, to converse with people we love; even the ability to perform the simplest and lowliest natural functions become, from this perspective, the greatest blessing.

Practical Poppycock

Pragmatic Sanctions

I have just been scanning the prefaces of two high school texts which are to guide the minds of our teen-agers in this community. The titles of the books: *English in Action* and *Chemistry in Action*. The clear implication of these titles and of the prefaces is that you must justify learning by relating it to something useful. You must learn English, dear children, because it's practical. It helps you write business letters and love letters and helps you to reply to your creditors in a most persuasive manner. You must learn chemistry because, well, chemistry is tied up with the atom bomb and the Nobel Prize, and you can com-municate better with others if you know the formula for green soap and methylene. The ultimate aim of learning is to make you a more skilful, successful, and well-adjusted social being, a happier communal sheep in the great sheep-fold, a more tractable ant in the cosmic heap, a more resigned and productive bee. The end of existence is to live together harmoniously like perfectly balanced billiard balls clicking softly against one another on vast green felt.

The Elliptical Ball

This practical view of learning is, I am happy to report, not the natural product of the student mind. The boys and girls with whom I deal have no such fusty opinion about why they are learning. The utilitarian philosophy in education is the thin mental ooze of those educators who are afraid to lose their jobs unless they can justify truth at the greasy counter of practicality. Only people unsure about their own relation to knowledge could feel such mousy insecurity about the right of schools to exist in their own right quite independent of their direct contribution to technical know-how, social engineering, national prosperity, or world peace.

Agile Midwife

We are told that the schools must produce harmonious social beings. Is this the primary task of the schools? Ants are social beings. So are hornets, beavers, and white corpuscles. By instinct and some rudimentary forms of habituation little hornets grow to behave like big hornets. But to be a man is to be something else. Man is free to be not only a harmonious billiard ball but an elliptical billiard ball, a screw ball, or an eight ball. He learns, not in order to actualize some common social potential but to actualize his own human and personal potential, to become through the beauty and terror, the loneliness and madness of his encounter with the truth, that which his destiny intends. To learn is to be born and to give birth. It is to be born and to be reborn a thousand times—to move from coziness into the coldness of the utterly new. The little child on his first day in kindergarten lets go of his mother's hand. He will do it again and again. He will find himself pushed toward the hostility of the strange, and he will live to see the strange become familiar. Even more secretive is what he discovers in himself. To learn is to give birth to ideas, a painful process in which the teacher functions merely as a respectful if agile midwife.

Now if learning is this complex process of development of the life and thought of an individual, the end cannot be some sort of pat social usefulness. Teachers are not called upon to be expert cookie cutters producing millions upon millions of gingerbread men with the currants in the right places. They are asked to assist at an initiation in which the curtain is pulled back upon truth and in which the initiate gropes for the steadying hand of someone who has been around.

The World's Coarse Thumb

I have been guilty through the years of some pretty dull teaching, and there have certainly been days on which my students had to console themselves with the promise of a grade or credits or a diploma while they spooned up the thin gruel of the lecture. But on less lazy or more inspired days I have seen ideas grip students in such a way that no one had to argue that the course was useful as an aid to salesmanship. In fact, so to argue would have been an intrusion upon esctasy—not, mind you, because the teacher was exceptional but because the true dimension of existence had been briefly glimpsed. A page from Dante or Milton or Dostoevski had worked an awareness of their destiny as men and women: half beast, half angel, the tarnished splendor for which Christ died. In that moment all that which, in Browning's words, "the world's coarse thumb and finger failed to plumb," was theirs.

On Travel

The Violet
Filter

On the eve of a rather important journey which will take us out of the country for several months, I should perhaps say something about travel. This is now such a common experience for Americans that we can no longer impress our friends with trunk stickers from Bagdad or colored slides from Corfu. Some of them have been there before us. Almost everyone is a Burton Holmes in mufti. It is not an uncommon experience for a professional lecturer to be told by an impudent listener, "Your pictures are O.K. but you over-exposed that shot of the Parthenon. I used Panchromatic XXX and a violet filter and I got a honey."

I Travel in
Concord

I shall not enter into the rather fruitless discussion about the broadening effect of travel. Does travel educate a man? No, say Emerson and Newman. Yes, say the travel agencies and certain college professors. Both Emerson and Newman wrote a hundred years ago. They had seen wealthy Yankees in Europe and sailors with parrots. They concluded that travel did not serve. I have seen thousands of American soldiers doing London and Paris with tourist thoroughness. I have seen them buy sofa pillows, terra cotta ash trays, and picture post cards of Stratford. Were they enriched? It would be snobbish to deny it. I think Emerson and Newman were probably bigger snobs than they cared to admit. They were bothered by the vulgarity and the spiritual torpor of the tourists they met. But like most intellectuals they probably overstated the case. The intellectual is not quite the pure spirit he thinks he is. And the ordinary man is not quite so porky as he is made out to be by the egghead.

I recall the disgust with which a friend of mine related an experience he had once had with some American tourists at Karnak. While he stood admiring the ancient temple ruins and heard within the footsteps of ghostly priests, the ladies in the party were discussing the evening menu in a loud voice, "Wasn't that a heavenly buffet last night? Almost like a Swedish *smörgåsbord*. And tonight there'll be steaks."

Such carnality is lamentable, and my friend was probably right when he insisted that money ought not give people a right to despise "the finer things" so conspicuously. But, on the other hand, are we so sure that people who discuss *gaffelbitar* at Karnak have missed the boat? Perhaps they were incapable by training and experience to understand Egyptian architecture. Perhaps they were unable to articulate what they felt, like a shy lover who expresses his ardor by discussing the weather. Or perhaps they were merely honest. In the midst of phony sophistication and feigned polish it is a relief to find an artlessness which is unafraid to speak the truth.

Pilgrim's
Progress

However the question is settled, we can probably conclude that both long hairs and short hairs, the erudite and the unlearned will continue to travel. They will ignore Newman and Emerson and head for the nearest ticket office. They were doing that when Paul boarded the Alexandrian grain ship and when Chaucer's pilgrims convened at the Tabard.

And the really overarching question is not what people get out of it in terms of immediate value: ideas, recipes, colored slides, anecdotes, and addresses. In all ages people have traveled for various immediate reasons. They did that in the Crusades and the pilgrimages of the middle ages. The big question is: Where are people going?

It is at this point that modern travelers differ from their ancestors who journeyed to Jerusalem and Canterbury and Campostello. In the fourteenth century the miscellany of pilgrims on their way to the shrine of Thomas a Becket could forget for a while that their goal was God. They could laugh and jest, connive and speculate, feast and flirt. But the day came when they must appear before the entombed saint and make their reckoning. This was the overarching fact.

It is not an overarching fact with modern travelers. The medieval pilgrims were tourists, but they were something more. Today we have mostly tourists. When they disembark, there is no shrine upon which they converge. To disembark is to diverge, forever to diverge.

This is what gives pathos to much of modern travel. For a tourist to go from New York to Liverpool and back again to New York is to go nowhere and with no one. But for a pilgrim all going is homegoing. The Apostle Paul leaves Jerusalem forever and goes home. Saint Birgitta leaves Sweden forever and goes home. David Livingstone presses into the tropical bush and goes home. And they go surrounded and sustained by the Innumerable Company.

On the Gilding of Lilies

Fried Bananas

In a fruit store the other day I began to think about bananas. When I was very young and in another country, we never thought about bananas in the plural. They came singly and with great rarity. Mother would go off to the city and when she came back there would be one banana for each of the four children. I wish I could convey the joy which the glimpse of that fruit gave us. Like the golden apples of Hesperides, the banana was something special. It did not belong in the category of apples and pears and plums, of blueberries and lingonberries and currants. Its position was not even challenged by the ravishing fragrance of wild strawberries or Malaga grapes. The banana came direct from the Garden of Eden. Eating it was a complicated ritual in which the four of us tried to extend the pleasure as long as possible. As I remember it, my brother always won the endurance contest. And I always lost. I was younger and less disciplined than he.

Then we came to America and one day in a paper I saw a recipe for *fried* bananas. It was the ultimate sacrilege. If bananas were perfection, why did they need to have anything done to them? To take that incarnation of jungled loveliness which was intended to be savored as a bee might sip a flower on a drowsy afternoon and to dump it into the smoking fat of a frying pan and render it greasy and formless was to violate its essence.

Electric Guitars

The bad side of technical initiative in America is that we feel we have to improve everything. Nothing is safe from our encroaching fingers. We electrify instruments. We take an indifferently good thing like the guitar, and we juice it up to sound like a seal's lament. And we transform a superior instrument like the pipe organ into something so mediocre as the electronic organ. We do the same to hymns. They can't be served up straight. They have to be fricasseed, basted, or boiled. Throw on a gob of mayonnaise and top it with a cherry. The excellent hymn "When I Survey the Wondrous Cross" comes out in an a la mode version with a bad tune and a sugary chorus. And simple, forthright hymn tunes have to be souped up with a shower of plinks in order to satisfy our tastes.

Parks With a Punch

The national parks are being treated to the same demand for an additive which will free sticky valves and give the motor added punch. People are no longer satisfied to see the miracle of Rocky Mountain National Park or Yosemite or Glacier. They want to combine the seeing with amusement parks, cocktail lounges, and stock car races.

111

Someone has suggested a ferris wheel on the edge of the Grand Canyon. The same site has been suggested for a huge elevator complex which would take people down to the floor of the canyon without the inconvenience of a donkey ride. During the summer I saw an ad for one of our numerous caves which promised all the comforts of home. A trip through the cave had now been enriched, read the ad, by electric lights, sanded walks, rest rooms, and Coca Cola machines at frequent intervals.

Look, but Don't Touch

It would be foolish to argue that life is always best when it is left in its natural state. I am not against what is usually termed progress. I believe that fire and cooking and the wheel and paved streets and inside plumbing and refrigeration are good things. And it is well to remember that most of these improvements have come about through the itch to tamper. What troubles me, I suppose, is the naive faith that everything can be bettered if we only fiddle with it long enough. There were people in the eighteenth century who rewrote Shakespeare. I have heard the suggestion that photography should replace oil painting; it does a better job. There was a New York minister who proposed that the proper attitude in church was not the bowed head and the bent knee but proud uprightness. Humility belonged to the middle ages. To all such crass innovators I would like to say what our parents said to us, "Look, but don't touch." There are some things which can be left as they are.

Time and the Timeless

Lund, Sweden

Tourists
Everlasting

The main attraction in Lund, the old cathedral and university city in southern Sweden, is not the 11th-century crypt or the 12th-century cathedral which unfolds in heavy Romanesque arches above it but the astronomical clock in the north aisle. Here every day at high noon gathers a miscellaneous crowd of school children, university students, farm women, and continental tourists. At the stroke of noon two horsemen in armor, surmounting the clock, clash brittle metallic lances in a ghostly joust. At the twelfth stroke, two trumpeters lift their horns, and to the strains of "In dulci jubilo" three wise men emerge from a door, circle the madonna and child, and disappear through another door which then closes on soundless hinges. It is an impressive performance even if it does not silence the tourists and the school children.

But now we have developed a tourist procedure which seems to function similarly in all situations. It consists of a half-attentive, half-neglectful flitting from object to ob-

113

ject, a restless refusal to be seriously involved in anything lest the next number get crowded out of the program. A tourist cannot allow himself the luxury of adoration or meditation or even of serious study. He munches, strolls, peers, whispers stagily, and worries his wrist watch. But he does not *attend*.

The astronomical clock is tailored to tourist needs. It provides brief, dramatic action in appropriate surroundings. It can be hurriedly noted, and, best of all, it can be left behind when its business is accomplished, without suggesting incompleteness and provoking feelings of guilt.

In Dulci Jubilo

If, however, you do not have to catch the bus to the next asterisk, you have time to remember that the clock was not made primarily as a doll's house or a mechanical toy, although it is both of these things. It was made as an aid to adoration. It suggests through the complexity of its mechanism (which notes not only the diurnal rhythm but the day of the year as well as the motion of the sun and moon) the primal fact that God is the God of space and time. And the fact is underscored by the sweetest and saddest of all the starry tales—the coming of the magi. The smooth course of the planet and the tortuous wanderings of men converge at last upon the Infant.

It is well to have this stated by the actions of mechanical dolls. A moving doll is a profound symbol of the fusion of time and the timeless. It is like those birds "which Grecian goldsmiths make of hammered gold and gold enamelling to keep a drowsy emperor awake or set upon a golden bough to sing to lords and ladies of Byzantium of what is past or passing or to come" (W. B. Yeats).

114

The dolls in the Lund horologium perform an action and thus enter the stream of time. In this they are like men—tourists and irritable visitors like myself. But they emerge from the waters of time unchanged, as we do not. The dolls have circled by one another and have turned to rest for 600 years. They still wear the same enchantingly empty expression. They still move with the same intriguing woodenness. We know that they will continue to do so. "Forever wilt thou love and she be fair," said Keats to the lovers carved on the Grecian urn. It is so with the dolls. They act, but they act without growing weary, without loss and pain. In this they speak not for what we are but for what we would like to be. And perhaps for what we shall be when we "shall serve Him night and day in His temple." The fragile nonchromatic notes of the music, "In dulci jubilo," reinforce the action. They suggest, as do the movements of the dolls, the joy of an absolute dedication to Christ the King. "To Him be honor and glory forever and ever. Amen."

Time Must Have
a Stop

Beneath the choir of the cathedral is the deep crypt in which all things come to a stop. It is the oldest part of the church, built well over 800 years ago. It is best to be alone down there and to taste, if only very briefly, the privation and loneliness of death. Here the dead lie locked in stone, the light filters sparingly, all sound is muted. But it has its own relevance. It is a tomb, of course. An inescapable finality. But it is also, through the miracle of Christian hope, the yet unquickened matrix of resurrected life. "In dulci jubilo."

115

Size, Speed, and Cost

The American
Caricature

The other evening we heard an illustrated lecture about Albert Schweitzer's great hospital at Lambaréne. The lecturer was a missionary doctor who had visited Schweitzer a few months ago and who for a few magic days had lived and worked side by side with the renowned humanitarian. The emphasis in the lecture was upon the extreme simplicity of the hospital at Lambaréne. It is apparently a huddle of tinroofed barracks without any pretension of sleek efficiency or comfort. The modern hospital bathed in cool light and with every sound muted by acoustic trickery, with polished corridors, gleaming chrome, and foam rubber mattresses, is unknown at Lambaréne. The wards are crowded, difficult of access, and insufferably hot and humid. The place swarms with all kinds of animal life from invalided gorillas to timorous mice. Every day under the direct supervision of Schweitzer the crudest kind of work is done on the grounds to hold back the invasion of the green chaos which always lurks on the edge of an equatorial plantation.

116

It is against this background that Schweitzer told one of his favorite anecdotes about the American journalist who recently asked him, "How much did Lambaréne cost?" "The Americans," said Schweitzer, "always ask how much a thing costs or how fast it goes." (Laughter)

America for Me

It may be that when an American goes overseas, he becomes unduly sensitive to jokes told at his country's expense. I am willing to grant that the laughter which greeted that caricature of Americans nettled me because I am at heart a flag waver and an unreconstructed provincial. But in addition to that I think it annoyed me because the association of America with quantity, price, and speed is both crude and false. It is crude because it assumes that these things are bad in themselves. It is false because it assumes that other people are not interested in these things, and worst of all, that this is all Americans think important.

Blessed Quantity

In the first place, we should begin to realize that the very nature of our civilization: its size, its complexity, and its interrelatedness require the very things which Americans are concerned about. The prissy idealist who mourns the invasion of bigness and speed without being aware of how much he depends on these very things should ask himself if he is willing to turn the clock back a few centuries. Is he willing to accept along with the age of Chartres and Rheims, the age of St. Francis and Dante, 12th-century plumbing and 13th-century hygiene? Even the noble Schweitzer, who

117

has paid an unbelievably high price to evade the corrupting touch of western civilization, uses his Nobel prize to buy new tin roofs for his hospital and has not, as far as I know, ever declined American dollars for his great work.

The Universal
Taint

In the second place, the assumption that only Americans like bigness is grossly in error. If you go to Russia, you are immediately shown the Gargantuan Russian subways, the gigantic universities, the vast and varied public parks. The same is true of such a relatively small nation as Sweden. The Swedes do not seem particularly modest about exhibiting their achievements in quantity. They will show you the "second largest single span bridge in Europe" with touching pride; they will take you to the spanking new Stockholm Subway; they will point to the immensity of the South Hospital, a complex of corridors and rooms both above and below ground which will accommodate 3,000 patients. Many Swedes can even give you without squeamishness the quantity of wood pulp exported annually.

Quantity Without
Quality

The unkindest cut of all, however, is the assumption, which is not uncommon here, that bigness is all Americans live for. This has led me to formulate the question, Where do we as Americans really live? Where are we most at home? Is it in size, in speed, in moneyed wealth? There is a great deal of this, of course. But isn't there also some evidence that what many Americans, if not most, want from life is the intimate and the unassuming? They want to live as families in the country or near it; they want to have friends; they want as the great overarching reality communion with God and an opportunity to share their means and their energies with people who need them. Americans want to live, in other words, where all people want to live —in the fulfilment of their destinies, not as automatons but as people, and perhaps as God's creatures.

A Right Jolly Old Elf

Uppsala, Sweden, a few days before Christmas

Syncretism in a Store Window

In a department store window here there is a large figure
in red pants and red jacket and black boots called *tomtefar*,
and his flabby rubber face grins and winks to the intense
delight of the children who waddle by in lumpy snowsuits
and heavy winter boots. The children know nothing about
syncretism and *cultural assimilation*, which imply the in-
grafting of one way of life upon another. They are very
young children and they cannot see that this is something
new in Swedish life—that the face is the face of the old
tomte who has lived on farms and upland steadings since
the dimmest antiquity but that the stature and the clothes
are the stature and the clothes of the American Santa
Claus. "The voice is Jacob's voice, but the hands are the
hands of Esau."

I think almost any amount of borrowing of American
folkways and American gadgets is allowable. But I do not
think that the Swedes ought to borrow Santa Claus.

Santa Claus and Christmas

I hasten to assure especially my younger readers that I have nothing against Santa Claus. I am for him. Christmas needs Santa Claus. The movement to put Christ back into Christmas has my full approval, of course. First things ought to come first. Christ is the Lord of Christmas, and to him belongs the glory and the prostrations of the billion-fold seraphic choir, the snowy wing tips and the glint of the golden circlets. To him belong also the first loyalties of little children. But Santa Claus has his place too. Somewhere behind the wise men and the shepherds and the donkey and the lamb, one should be able to glimpse his comfortable figure.

I once heard of a well-meaning person who banished Santa Claus from a children's Sunday school party. The old boy didn't belong in church, she said. He was secular and of disputable origin and anyway the church belonged to the Lord. I honor the lady's sincerity, but I question her theology. The earth is the Lord's and the fullness thereof and to Christ belong the wonder and the terror, the anguish and the mystery of time. He has put on time like a vesture. History is his. The myth and the legend, the cradle song and the love song, the fairy tale and the proverbs, the tired wisdom of tired old brains and the fresh dream which lies like a blade of sunlight across the land—all, all are his. And it is not at all a contradiction that the medieval churches built into their walls and towers, their windows and their sculpture, a whole gallery of figures—a heritage of the pre-Christian past. The medieval church took over an old culture and conquered it, not by destroying it but by baptizing it to holy uses. You see traces of it all over this land, not only in gargoyles and other mysterious figures carved in churchly stone but in other christened usages. The old temple site became the place where the Christian church was built; the sacrificial grove became a church yard; the pagan well, a source of water for worship and worshippers.

As a beam of light becomes engaged in stained glass and blooms into richness of color and form, so Christ engaged himself in the fullness of human existence. He brightened it with meaning. There is even an old tradition that he harrowed Hell. Certainly the Lord of Hell is Christ's reluctant prisoner. I can't believe that he is too fearful of Santa Claus.

A New Baptism

However, what the Swedes need more than to adopt our Santa Claus is to resubmit their civilization to baptismal grace—to Americanize less and to Christianize more. There are spanking new developments in the cities with thousands of apartments glistening in tile and chrome and stainless steel where the church of Christ cannot go in force. The State Church is trapped in an unwieldy system which does not permit flexibility and speed of movement, and the free churches are hampered by a lack of finances and of personnel. Much is being done of course, and credit should go to those who wage the battle. But much more must be done if Sweden is not to become once more a shrine of heathendom.

Justice in a Christmas Card

Uppsala, a few days before Christmas

Sentiment and
Judgment

It has been a strange experience to find, among all the Christmas sentiments which have descended upon us, this velvet-smooth and scented snowfall of rose petals, a word piercing as a bee sting. It came on a mimeographed sheet which was tucked into a quite conventional greeting card envelope. It said:

Free me, O Jesus, from the desire to be appreciated.
Free me, O Jesus, from the desire to be loved.
Free me, O Jesus, from the desire to be sought after.
Free me, O Jesus, from the desire to be honored.

It said a great deal more, but this was enough. There rose out of the sickening pain of the words (a prayer by Cardinal Merry del Val) not only a concept but an image of the Lust for Appreciation. And in the center of the image there was a person well-known to me.

Lord Bountiful

The image was a couple of decades old. It floated up from the depression years, the depression Christmases. I was a young assistant pastor in a large parish and it was my job to direct the distribution of Christmas baskets to the *poor*. I remember the gaiety which marked our venture into charity. I was very young and very green, and I was assisted by a rosy-cheeked band of youths and maidens. I recall with what concentration of egotistical feelings I approached the first unpainted shack. I rang the bell and when we were invited in, I marched like a laurel-crowned victor at the head of a procession of canned tomatoes, charity hams, and Delicious apples. When we reached the kitchen, we set our easy burden down before the assembled family. Then we waited for what we were sure would be an outburst of tearful adult gratitude mingled with the happy gurgles of children. There was nothing. We were ringed round by stony silence, which is what we deserved.

But we learned nothing. We were secure in our self-esteem and attributed the response we got to the churlishness of the objects of our goodness. And we continued on our way on Operation Bountiful, scintillating with benevolent canned goods and radiating our own brand of pious conceit.

Scrooge in Reverse

One of the traditions in our family is the annual playing of a recording of Dickens' *Christmas Carol*. We shall miss that little ritual this year. But I must confess that although

Dickens speaks to my heart, he fails to convince my moral judgment.

The unrepentant Scrooge is sound enough and so is the Scrooge who in his absurd nightcap twists and groans before the Christmas ghosts. But the morning-after Scrooge with all his frantic projects of jollification strikes me as a man who has merely exchanged one sort of greed for another. In his miserable unheated office he grasped for gold; on the morning of his redemption he reaches out eagerly for appreciation and approval.

The Bitter
Fact

The Christian faith nowhere teaches that generosity is the essence of morality or that a reversal from doing a particular sort of evil to doing a particular sort of good is what is meant by salvation. The primary experience of the Christian life is neither reform nor conversion in any shallow sense. It is death. And it is only in death that our pathetic efforts to *do good* are seen for what they really are: the scramble to be liked, to be sought after, to be, perhaps, adored.

There is a peculiar species of pride which is so subtle that it is frequently confused with generosity. It is the pride which will never be served because it wants to function as the servant. It is the pride which always wants to be host and never guest, or, if guest, then the most disengaged and distrait of these. So that it shall seem that the acceptance of the invitation and not the giving of it is the truly generous act. The way in which we sometimes humor children by drinking their poor tepid lemonade and appearing to like it hugely.

There was none of this in Jesus and precious little of it in his apostles. Can we imagine a Jesus who would say to himself, "I must really trot down to Bethany a bit. Not that I enjoy it, but it makes the blokes feel better"? Or an Apostle Paul who did the imperial circuit in order to stand well in a Popularity Poll?

The Day Burning Like an Oven

Uppsala, Sweden

The Unendurable
Fact

Despite scientific training and the creation of an atmosphere of "objectivity" in which we are supposed to be able to think and talk about anything without embarrassment, we live our lives within the padding of an illusion. We not only believe but need to believe in facades and appearances in order to maintain our sanity. To be truly disillusioned in the ghost and dream world in which we live is to suffer the most excruciating pain. To live for a moment in the absolute truth is to experience the Last Judgment, for "Who can endure the day of His coming and who can stand when He appears, for He is like a refiner's fire and like fullers' soap."

My first experience of the terror of disillusionment came in a butcher shop in a little Pennsylvania town. I was employed as a shop assistant, which meant that I had a miscellany of duties. I sliced up the beautiful pink boiled ham and the red summer sausage on the slicing machine. I plunged into the vast walk-in cooler at the back of the shop for such sections of beef and veal and pork as I could manage. I delivered innumerable packages of meat. In the evening I scrubbed the cutting blocks with a wire brush and I swept up the sawdust from the floor and replaced it with new.

It was a pleasant job for the summer. I was somewhere between thirteen and fourteen, and I would much rather have been outside playing basketball and baseball or gone swimming or just loafed around the high-ceilinged, cool, old town library which was strong on Mrs. Southworth and Grace Livingston Hill and weak on Dreiser and Sinclair Lewis. But as a job it had its advantages. Now and then I was allowed "to wait on the trade." I could grind hamburger and cut round steak and wrap and make change and smile engagingly and act grown up and competent. And then there was the butcher. He was a sturdy and somewhat squat German with a florid face and golden hair receding at the temple. He attributed the rosiness of his complexion to the custom of drinking beef blood at a slaughter house in which he had served his apprenticeship. He insisted that this was a time-worn usage among German butchers, and I believed and marvelled. And he had a tongue like a golden needle. Out of the poor little snippets of his ordinary life he could verbally stitch together and embroider fabrics of infinite richness and diversity. He was without any sort of education and this may have accounted for his lack of self-consciousness. He narrated, he described, he dramatized, he exaggerated, distorted, and lied. He was, like most of the employers I had had even at that tender age, foul-mouthed, but I have no recollection that this particularly affected me. Children at that age have their own armor of pudicity and detachment. But what did impress me was his power to conjure up a world I never knew of exitement and adventure.

The annual Butchers' Picnic was scheduled for a day in August at an amusement park in a nearby town and this became for several weeks the focus of my employer's interest and the subject of his fantasies. Before my astounded eyes he painted a paradisal picnic in which at his expense I would move from roller coaster to Old Mill to Fun Fair to the Whip without any interruption. In transit there would be the buying and consuming of hot dogs, ice cream cones, Cracker Jack, and candy bars. I would swim in pop. I would sink down, be submerged, and drown in pure pleasure.

Who Can Stand When
He Appears?

The Picnic Day came. It was clear, calm, and sunny. I was to meet my employer at the ticket booth in West View Amusement Park. Dressed in my best white duck pants and a white shirt, I arrived at the rendezvous point a half hour early. I waited. I looked at my Ingersoll wrist watch and saw the luminous minute hand crawl across the black face. It nudged up to the top of the dial while I cast anxious looks over the faces of the assembling butchers. Five minutes went by. Ten. Fifteen. At 2:30 he had not come. I waited until 3. And until 3:30. I made up excuses for him. There had been a flat tire. His wife had burned the meatballs. He had misunderstood the time. But as the precious afternoon crept by and I made wider and wider excursions from the ticket booth, I began to understand that I had been fooled.

129

The next morning I said ever so shyly that I must have missed him at the park. I don't remember his answer, but I remember the impression it made on me of naked and pitiable falsehood. In my childish eyes the hero was unmasked for once and for always.

And yet, and this is the mystery, when he began not long after to spin his golden yarn, I listened and was enthralled. So desperately do we cling to our illusions.

An Inheritance Incorruptible

Uppsala, Sweden

The Noble
Savage

In Jukkasjärvi, near the mountain-born headwaters of the great Torne River, an island of unspoiled Lapp culture remains. The bus comes out daily from Kiruna and you can buy Stockholm papers and Marabou chocolate bars at the little newsstand, but the cemetery is still located across the river (to keep restive ghosts at a distance) and you can meet a pure species of Lapp in whom old paganism, Lutheran piety, and Laestadian frenzy have mingled into something monumental and aloof.

Like all American tourists I brought my camera to Jukkasjärvi. (There will be winter nights in Chicago when a few discreet slides can be perpetrated on guests between the last fresh anecdote and the fruit salad.) The old church from the 1600s was quite passive while I fiddled with exposure speeds and a new film cartridge. But after the "still life" I tried to catch mobile life. A boy of ten, splendid in new Lapp attire: blue and red and gold, shot by on his "spark." (The "spark" is a characteristic Scandinavian sled

131

which looks like a chair on steel runners and which is propelled by being kicked.) In addition to all his other glory, he had shiny new boots. He would have been good "human interest" for my film lecture. I could hear the appreciative "ahs" from my otherwise sluggish audience. I waved cheerily like a politician at a whistle stop and asked if I could take his picture. He howled a Lapp negation and kicked his sled faster. Then I became even more audacious. "A crown," I shouted at his retreating finery, "I'll give you a whole crown!" But from under his magnificent tassel no sound proceeded but a shrieked "Na-a-a-a-j!" He was gone with a flash of steel and a glimmer of boot leather.

Not for Sale

I don't know what dark motives churned under his splendidly tufted cap. Shyness, hoary *tabu* (a camera has the evil eye which may strike with madness or with death), Laestadian prejudice (a picture of oneself is a form of wicked egotism like looking in a mirror). I don't know the source of his aversion. But whatever it was, I honor him. He stuck to his pop gun in the face of crunchy chocolate bars and glittering pieces of silver.

The Oil of Gladness

I have told myself that such unswerving refusal to compromise is an impossibility in any society. Theoretically I am forced to agree with the hangdog political realism of T. V. Smith. According to this doctrine, politics is a species of horse trading. For the sake of getting my bill on new housing passed, I soften up and vote for a blubber refinery at Bloated Bay which my opponent wants but I do not. I buy and I sell. That is, I buy others and I sell myself. That is politics.

It is, woe is me, also church politics. I know my friends, and I reward them. But I also know my opponents and am known of them. For the sake of something or other Herod and Pilate became friends *that day.* So insubstantial, so cloud-like but, ah, so real are the issues of compromise! And out of such gossamer is the solid horse blanket of politics woven! Even at the Biennial Clam Bake of the Only True Church of God the loom is busy. The fraternal (i.e., political) spirit flows down like oil in the beard of Aaron.

Te Deum
Laudamus!

And because things are like this in our vale of tears and to grow older means to lose the fine edge of the pure negation, to lose the lion's teeth and to roar through harmless gums, I say hats off to the Lapp boy! Hats off to his impertinence, to his flailing feet, to his wild flight. And hats off to that missionary saint who once wrote out of some deep wellspring of wrath, "To Hell with your church politics!" Once in a while the devil ought to have the inkwell smack in his leering face.

"This is my body..."

The Sugary
Collective

One of my pet ideas, well known to my students, who have seen it trotted out often enough, and to my friends, who can herald its approach in my conversation by a certain fluttering of my nostrils, is the *bodily* character of the church. For me the church is not a collection of souls but an organic unity of particular people with faces and bodies and dispositions who through the miracle of grace manage to love one another—almost.

The other day I got an angry letter with a legitimate beef. The writer was objecting to my over-evaluation of the church. He felt that I had made it into an exclusive Kozy Klub for the likeminded. He felt that the whole thing smelled oversweet like pomade. He was right and I was wrong. I had been guilty of what in psychological language is called the "overevaluation of the beloved object."

Now I read that Simone Weil, a convert to Christianity, has spoken out against collective experience in her book

Waiting for God, recently published in Sweden. I quote a paragraph from a review:

> The criticism of the church is for Simone Weil a criticism of all collectives. Collective existence is for her a demonic temptation—it is possible that the collectivism of the Nazis has played a role in determining her feeling. She loathes the collective feeling, the experience of sweetness in the bosom of the group; for her it is a dangerous substitute for faith and the church frequently offers this substitute.

I am reminded of Elinor Wylie's stanza:

> *. . . . shun the polluted flock*
> *Cling like that noble bird,*
> *The eagle, to the rock.*

I am reminded of Elinor Wylie and Kierkegaard and Nietzsche.

Kozy Klub

Let us give them their due. What all of these people object to in the *collective* is a real peril for the human spirit. It is the subhuman collective to which they object: the beehive, the ant heap. They prefer the freezing aloneness of the mountaintop to the warm furry togetherness of the herd. And let us in all conscience admit that the church has often become just such an inbred and inbreathing fraternity—a parochial pond on which all the little ducklings quack alike.

Undoubtedly the church ministers most effectively to us

ordinary ducklings. The individualists, the introverts, the eggheads, we have labeled "ugly." We have made them feel that to be a Christian means to be "conformed by the re-doing of one's mind" and to adopt our pattern of taste, broadloom, blue tile, and bathos.

His Body

This is all very sad because although the church is a body, that is, a living togetherness into which are poured all our lovable and unlovely idiosyncracies, it is not *our* body. An organism through which we transmit our collective itches and urges. It is *His* body. And this makes all the difference. For then the church is not a sounding board for my personal melody but a means of transforming my thin little tremulo into an orchestration. (I recognize the triteness of this trope, but beg indulgence.)

Simone Weil fears "sweetness in the bosom of the group," but the body of Christ, when it is true to its essence, offers no such seductive sweetness. What it offers through divine grace is an opportunity to identify ourselves redemptively with the sinning and the suffering. "To complete what is lacking in Christ's affliction for the sake of his body which is the church," writes Paul. This is audacious, for it implies that the church may die for the world as Christ once died for us, becoming in truth his crucified body.

Concrete Crucifixion

These high words will have about them the hollow ring of a political assurance unless we understand what they really mean. They mean the sort of earthly, everyday, practical concern for our neighbor's blessedness (I don't say "happiness" for the two are not synonymous) which will prompt us to accept the invitation of his need. The highest courage is not to teach the sick to accept their sickness. The highest courage is to nerve the will of the sick to want wholeness. It is then virtue goes out of us. To fill up the sufferings of Christ is, through grace, to pour our life into the dying. So that, as the blessed apostle says, "death is at work in us, but life in you." Amen. So be it.

"He who digs a pit..."

Uppsala, Sweden

The Mills of
the Gods

For years now I have had my little private joke about the entertainment value of colored slides. Since the advent of the "candid camera" some twenty years ago, the western world has teemed with amateur photographers who, unlike their modest ancestors, have ambitions to succeed Burton Holmes. They have swooped down on national parks and monuments, on beauty spots and scenic views, on relatives and notables with the intense concentration of bees gathering honey. And they have winged their way home laden with pictorial sweetness, encapsulated sunshine for the dull days of winter.

Then in fading October and sullen November the honeycombs have been trotted out. Just as the conversation is rising above the banality of weather and the threat of a local sausage factory, the host clears his throat as for a major speech and says, "I have a few slides we took last summer. Nothing professional, you know. Inexpensive equipment and no fancy lecture. Thought you might be interested."

Among the guests then there is the faintest murmur of interest fringing a stupefied silence. But no response is needed. The projector is already being wheeled into place, the slide boxes lugged in, the screen unrolled. The guests get out of their chairs and with the gray patience of Indian elephants rolling a teak log, they push their chairs into place before the silver screen.

The Slow
Grind

There used to be a time when the photography was so poor and the projector so unreliable that you could indulge in comic relief. When the slide of Uncle August came in upside down or underexposure made identification impossible, there might be a little ripple of amusement. It wasn't very funny, but it was something. But now everything is technically perfect. And deadly. The slides are fed in automatically from long plastic trays which hold an indecent number of pictures. They are air-cooled and cleaned with perma-mist and they spray the screen with the chilling regularity of a burp gun burst. You get the World War II Victory monument in the square of Spoleto, Zugreb, Pinsk, Al Hazir, Jubjow, Schlichtenstein, Puteoli, Miscolc, and Prut. And you get it from all four directions plus N NW and you get in 18 din Agfacolor 100/5.6 and an hour later with Kodachrome 100/11, 21 din which gives you the blue and red values a little better. You get the Spanish folk dancers and the church boats on Siljan and the modern apartment buildings in Stockholm, and the Parthenon (overexposed), and the changing of the guard at Buckingham Palace (it rained so we managed to pick up some slides at a camera shop), and the bears in Yellowstone Park, and the girls in Cypress Gardens, and a grinning Indian by a cactus in New Mexico, and a grinning Mexican by a cactus in Mexico. The colored tide, smooth as river oil and bewildering as a visit to a plaid mill, washes against you, over you, and through you. After the 700th slide the nerve endings are screaming. You look around. On every face there is occupational pallor and a fringe of sweat along the upper lip. On every face except that of the exhibitor. There you read only exhilaration.

Falls Himself
Therein

This, as I say, was my private joke. Until a few months ago. Then one fateful night I rented a projector, herded some folks together, and began, "I have a few slides. . . ." As I flipped through slide after slide, the clarity, brightness, and composition of my photography delighted me. I felt ecstasy mounting within me. Terrific! Great! Then it happened. In a momentary lull I heard a child yawn. Unmistakably. But it couldn't be. These slides couldn't bore anyone. How could they? They were *mine*.

Content in Fire

Stockholm, Sweden

Constructive Criticism

There is a fiction among tolerant and poised people that the distaste for criticism can be overcome like the aversion for castor oil. I have heard some of them say as they submitted their work for comment and criticism, "Don't hesitate to give this thing the business. I know it's poor in spots, and furthermore I *like* constructive criticism." I don't believe it. I don't believe that anyone likes to have himself or his work criticized even if it is done constructively, even if it is done in love. We may see the need for critical surgery. We may convince ourselves that all great men have had their works scrutinized. We may want very much to attain that nobility which is unruffled by an adverse judgment. We may even be able to smile outwardly while the scalpel cuts. But we do not *like* it. Let us not kid ourselves. The attack upon us even by incompetent and vicious people leaves us shaken.

I recall a conversation I once had with a young second lieutenant. Both of us had definite opinions about modern literature and the exchange became rather heated. But I forgot the matter promptly. Several years later I ran into the same officer at the University of Chicago. He remembered our discussion. In fact, he remembered it too well. "You were terribly caustic," he said; "you may have been right but you were a lot rougher than you needed to be."

I didn't tell him that the blows I had struck were born of desperation. I had felt my own position assailed and I had fought for my life.

The Castle of
Illusion

Those who reckon only with man's rational nature sometimes forget that all of us spend considerable energy building and inhabiting a dream house. Into its walls and roof-tree go all the nice things that people say to us and about us. Praise, commendation, flattery, approval are greedily gathered in and put to use. Into this building pass also our own happy self-deceptions, our rosy estimates of ourselves, the giddy memories of our infrequent triumphs.

Perhaps it is unjust to say that this cozy cottage is all illusion. We are certainly good for something. The house we live in has a few sound timbers and a few tiles which are not cracked. But it is not what in our happy fancy we imagine it to be.

Destructive
Criticism

Now the pathos of all this is that even when we have lived in our little straw house for many years and have patched it and buttressed it to the best of our ability, *we remain unconvinced.* We awaken in the night and wonder what huff or what puff may blow us down. We scan the heavens for a sign of disaster. We are like a man who has embezzled funds and who waits for the audit.

That is why criticism affects us so deeply. However slight, it rocks our dream house. It insinuates a doubt into the belief that we are godlike. Let someone suggest that we have split an infinitive, retold an anecdote badly, made a slightly unfavorable impression on a new acquaintance, muffed the ball in one of a hundred routine assignments, and we howl inwardly. Sweat forms at the temples. We lie staring at the plaster and project an expedition to an obscure Pacific atoll. We wonder with Hamlet whether it is best to be or not to be.

Content in Fire

Dante speaks of those on the terrace of love in purgatory as "content in fire." To be content in the fire of criticism is impossible for us ordinary people. We may stoically admit the need of the fire, but it doesn't content us. To live with such a sense of divine purpose in the midst of the fire that we are satisfied to be there and nowhere else is a gift of divine grace. But it is a gift for which we certainly ought to pray, assisted in our petition by that Spirit of Truth which because of the magnitude of our resistance prays for us with "unutterable groanings."

Nature and Culture

Skåne, Sweden

Optimum Conditions

I have finally found the sort of Arcadia one dreams about in projecting a book: a sleepy rural hamlet where the railroad trains to Malmö are an event. The house in which I live is not ancient but it is pervaded by an ancient culture. There is no telephone, no TV, and the radio speaks infrequently and softly like a well-mannered woman. I have a room on the second floor and except for a duo of incredibly cranky children in the next house, nothing disturbs the routine of writing. Here there are no electric vacuum cleaners, no noisy plumbing, not even a humming refrigerator. Only the electric lights proclaim the fact that we are in the twentieth and not in the seventeenth century.

Outside my window I can see the wood-shed and the well where water is winched up. Under the house is the cellar where food is kept cool. In the distance there is a sun-warmed pavilion, the restful antiquity of which defies tile and chrome and sunken Tiberian baths.

144

Between
Paragraphs

When inspiration ceases, I walk in the woods. There is an uncle who lives nearby. His mind and his attic are crammed with miscellaneous facts and artifacts: anecdotes, superstition, and folk wit are jumbled together with copper coffee pots, shuttles, butter crocks, brass tubas, muzzle loaders, and a gallery of art in lithograph so incredibly bad that I can feel only awe. Pale maidens swoon on tombstones, kittens don muffs and spectacles and tip the ink well, a German duke bestrides a horse and looks out from bales of whiskers upon nothingness. Then there are the books in black imitation leather bindings and German script with yellowed pages smelling of stale—unread books passing from father to son or from aunt to nephew as "books," that is, as culture property but not as vehicles of ideas.

Hieroglyph
of Hoof

We walk *through* the woods on the way home from haying. In his world one does not walk *in* the woods on week days. One walks with a purpose: either to the fields or from the fields. And the road cuts through the woods. Here there is event but no history. Leave the woods to themselves and you get green ebb and flood but no noticeable change. They don't go anywhere. By my foot I see a long speckled shape. I start. "A viper skin," he says. "There's plenty of them this year. And there's elk." He points with an old finger that is gnarled like a twig at fresh indentations in the moss. "You can see it isn't a cow. Elk have a different kind of hoof."

We pass places in the forest road where the ants have burrowed. We see deer tracks in the moist sand by a spring. A woodland meadow is half-choked now with young spruce

"It needs to be retiled," he says, "and the trees should be cleared away, but it don't pay. So we let the woods take over." And the woods will. In the decades which have passed since I was here as a child the green tide has pushed itself in. A tarn where we skated is filled in now and overgrown. A glade where heather grew is young forest. A knoll we called the "Mountain" is covered with a heavy growth of timber. Here and there the crofts stand desolate, the little houses are falling into ruin. Grass has choked the well, the garden beds, the cow shed. Soon the forest will be back. Maple and fir will root under the kitchen floor and growing spars will soar upwards through the rib cage of roof tree and rafter. In a generation —and what is a generation in the forest?—the trees will join over the ruins and the moss will come and do its reconciling work.

Unresigned

Nature has its power and its beauty. It has its inevitability and rhythm. Elks ebb and flow. Vipers ebb and flow. Hazelnuts and apples, lemmings and lilacs are plentiful and scarce. There is a way in which all of us share in this mysterious rhythm: the skin, the hair, the blood, the tissues, the organs—all live within the motion of sun and moon.

It is well to know this kinship with nature: to see ourselves as one with the rest of creation. But it is also well not to be resigned in the face of it. We are not Mowglis and Tarzans or *only* that.

We are beings capable of culture and of history. Human life is not a succession of endless cycles; it is a vast drama with a beginning, a middle, and an end. And through it we move not as elks and vipers but as creatures burdened and dignified with the terror of choice.

Summer Scapegoat

Sweden

She Ain't What
She Used to Be

This year, as in all years I can remember, people are complaining about the weather. When it's warm, it's too warm; when it rains, it is an unusually wet summer. The words *unusual, strange, peculiar, out-of-the-ordinary* occur frequently in conversation. It's like the talk about the younger generation. "The kids who are going to high school seem smaller than ever—and ornerier. I don't say we were angels, but this modern generation . . ." And money. "It doesn't buy anything any more. Now when we were young, you could buy a pie for twenty-five cents; a haircut was two bits; there were two-cent ice-cream cones."

What is one to conclude from all this breast-beating, this mewling in a minor key? That people are constitutionally unpleasant and querulous? Absurd. We know that most people are not fretful at all and that when the going

148

is rough, most human beings manage to be amazingly cheerful and patient.

Search for the Wonderful

I have a theory that people react as they do to weather, youth, and inflation because they dread boredom. Few of us manage to be articulate unless we are negative. To praise something requires energy and imagination which most of us do not want to cultivate. And so when the great boring silence moves in upon us, we defend ourselves by lining up as many gripes as we can think of and then firing them off.

Bickering between married people belongs in this category. What escape from boredom lies in the discovery of and the enlargement upon a connubial weakness. How many marriages have been rendered happy and permanent because the husband had a habit of snoring or the wife was gifted with an unpleasant voice! How these subjects can be embroidered, discussed over the telephone, deliberated upon in the night watches! From such excitement divorce does not come. Divorce rears its ugly head when all the tension is over—when anger had died and irritation withered and only cold boredom watches the hours drip in the stained sink.

The wonderful may also live in political opposition. How much amusement and flight from the ordinary the Democrats have furnished the Republicans! How thankful the Democrats should be for the late Senator McCarthy and the Republicans for Henry Wallace! What pleasant throbbing of blood and buzzing of ear their very existence has wrought!

The Spoil
Sport

Hence it is futile and perhaps injurious to try to convince people that things are not so bad as they think. I have noticed that efforts to prove that the weather this year is about normal, that young people are no better and no worse than ever, that our inflated prices have brought higher wages—all these efforts encounter suspicion and hostility. People want things to be wonderful even if they are wonderfully bad.

I have also noted that they want wonderful *causes*. Most Swedes seem to want to believe that we have bad weather this year and that the bad weather is *caused* by American atomic tests. Meteorologists do not believe that atomic fission can have anything to do with global weather. They say that proportionately an atom blast is like a flea's cough. But this people do not want to believe. It is much more thrilling to believe the weather is caused by American militarism than by spots in the sun.

It's the same with disease. To believe that disease is caused by an invasion of viruses or bacilli is much too ordinary. But to believe that it comes from something my mother saw when I was yet in the lower parts of the earth or from a dislocation of my clavicle—that is truly wonderful and believable and right.

And so with cures. A cure must be wonderful too. It cannot be gradual and understandable. It must be sudden and marvelous. It must come from an incantation, a mystical poke in the solar plexus, a glittering gadget. We are fearfully and wonderfully made, and we are made so that we cannot live unless we are nourished with the marvelous.

Brideshead Revisited

Frankfurt/Main, Germany

Rip Van Winkle

After an absence of twelve years I am back in Germany. I have not, like the legended Winkle, slept away the years. With the average American I have followed developments here in *Life* magazine. Gaps in the briefing have been filled in by tourist lectures illustrated with colored slides. But despite this orientation I was not prepared for what I have seen since the SAS plane dropped me at Rhine-Main Airfield a few days ago. When I last saw this part of Germany, it was rubble. Everything served military purpose. There were roads, but they were jammed with military vehicles, burned-out equipment, and tired men. There were houses, but they were either empty or served as military headquarters. The civilians were fearful and confused. They had been given the script for a successful adventure story but something had gone haywire in the fourth act.

151

Noisy Bells Be
Dumb

Easter Saturday, 1945, I was in a column grinding north from Darmstadt. North and east of us in the vicinity of Gelnhausen there were occasional puffs of sound. We moved past destroyed German vehicles. Under the trees nestled the skeletons of burned German fighter planes. A pale sun washed the wide concrete highway. The column stopped. The sound from Gelnhausen increased in tempo and thickened. Baker Company was having trouble. Someone was always having trouble. To ease the tension you dismounted, walked back and forth, kicked the greening turf.

An officer came down the highway with a Special Services paperbound book in his hand. It was egg yellow. "Just having some Housman," he said. "Pretty bitter guy, isn't he? You noisy bells be dumb, I hear you, I will come." "Bitter and not a Christian," you said, "but maybe the kind of poet for this kind of day." And you thought of all the ways that Death sang in Housman and all the ways that Death and only Death spoke to you today in the midst of this pale sun and this new green. The day of the buried Christ. The day of the vermilion star spreading in the pale forehead of the soldier facing the steely gun and the graygreen claws of the tank which comes and comes and will not stop. You noisy bells be dumb, I hear you, I will come.

Vanity Fair

Now all this is over and out of the rubble, phoenix-like, rises the airy structure of a new world: aluminum, stainless steel, wide panes of crystal glass, brilliant enamelled panels of azure and scarlet. A new city poised like a seraph over the darkling world. And where a few years ago the columns groped through dark streets with only the blackout lights peering like nearsighted eyes into nothingness there is now a cascade of neon telling you about the joy of Mercedes-Benz and the joy of the DKW and the joy of television.

The other night here in Frankfurt I went to see a Radio-Television Exposition put on by a group of German manufacturers. It was dazzling, deafening, and breath-taking. *Der Grossen Deutschen Rundfunk-, Fernseh- und Phono-Ausstellung 1957.* I counted over a dozen brand names in German television, all with vast areas of floor space and all with the very latest in electronic devices, model designs, and sales technique. There were TV sets, radios, tape recorders, phonographs, and new recording devices without number served up with a sauce of fluorescent lighting, rock gardens, falling water, and lithographed publicity which made me feel like the Primal Rube on his first visit to the Claybottom County Fair.

Operation World-Wide

With German thoroughness, technical knowhow, and obsessive delight in contrivances, this once prostrate people has climbed to the top of the technical heap in a matter of months. American capital has helped, but there are good and bad stewards. The Germans deserve credit for not having buried their talents. German city life today looks like city life elsewhere in the world. Outwardly the Germans have hidden the scars of the war under the standardized garment of urban culture which is common to a thousand cities from Stockholm to Sidney.

Who Lives Here?

The intriguing question to which I have found no answer anywhere in my walks and talks, my reading and my listening, is this: Who lives in this new house? When you ring the chimes to the ultra-modern apartment, who opens the door? It is a question to which a foreigner can find no easy answer. It may be the kind of question which the Germans themselves have not yet been able to answer. And yet in the answer to that question lies the future of Europe and perhaps of the world.

The Hatred of Theologians

Sweden

Nygren vs. Wingren

We have been treated the past months to the unedifying spectacle of theologians in the heavyweight class having a go at one another. In a quarterly journal Sweden's most renowned theologian, Bishop Nygren, the fount of *agape**
theology, has been venting his spleen on a younger but no less wrathful colleague, Professor Wingren. By now the match has reached the 14th round, the participants are clinching repeatedly, the referee is asleep, and the spectators have gone home. The only difference between this bout and the Patterson-Rademacher fight is that in the latter the combatants shook hands before and after their battle. But theologians deal with too spiritual a subject matter to descend to such trivial courtesies. They are content to shake their fists at one another and to roar.

Meanwhile one hears from Switzerland that the ancient city of Basel is not large enough for Karl Barth and Oscar

---

* *Agape* is unmotivated love, the classic example being God's love for sinners.

Cullman, two internationally famous pachyderms in the theological menagerie.

Queen of the Sciences

Now theology is a holy science and we ought to honor the men who have so high an opinion of her excellence that they are willing to depress the skulls of those who would besmirch her. Thus Athanasius defended the unity of substance in the Godhead, Leo fought for the two natures of Christ, Augustine for depravity, Anselm for the incarnation, Luther for the substantiality of the supper, Calvin for infant baptism, and P. P. Waldenstrom for an unchanging God in the atonement, and all of these men surrounded themselves with the recumbent bodies of their foes: Arius, Pelagius, Zwingli, Servetus, and others. The thought of what would have happened if these bloody corpses had triumphed fills the mind with horror.

Down With the Protestants

Theological hate expresses itself in other ways. Just now some younger Lutherans and Anglicans are disclaiming the connection of their churches with Protestantism. The Anglicans want to skip the Reformation entirely and call themselves Catholics against the apoplectic protests of the Roman Church. And the new Lutherans are so enthusiastically *Lutheran* that the common protest of the reformers against Roman abuses is being more and more soft-pedalled. An extreme form of this Luther worship is found in a recent scholarly study of the great reformer where the writer speaks of "Luther before he became a Lutheran." The idiocy of this formulation is so wonderful that the words could well be inscribed as a motto on the standards of the elect. What it suggests is that there existed from all eternity a theological system called Lutheranism which the monk Martin Luther, when he came to his senses, was smart enough to embrace.

Now the fact is, and sober church historians will admit it, that there is no such thing as Lutheranism. The Augsburg confession is not "Lutheran" nor is the formula of Concord. Luther's views on the Scriptures, on law and grace, on the church, on free will, were never systematically elaborated. What one finds in Luther is not a system but a way of looking at theological questions so paradoxical, so impassioned, so intuitive, that to lay Luther beside the dogmatics which bear his name is like comparing El Greco's paintings with those of Plockhorst.

What the young men seem to mean when they set "Lutheran" over against "Protestant" is not so much the Luther of the Diet of Worms as the Luther of a later period—the defender of church art against the iconoclasts, the architect of the German mass, the opponent of Zwingli and the Anabaptists. They want a Luther who smiles benignly at their altar service, their vestments, candles, chants, signs of the cross, genuflections, elevations, hand lavings.

Here I Stand!

But there is a nobler community than that of the vested prelates. It is the communion of men and women, Anglican, Calvinist, Lutheran, and Anabaptist, who once in angry protest against a church which had betrayed its trust rang the great bell of the Reformation: "Let God be God." It was because of them that the Bible became again a living book.

Let the younger Lutherans and the younger Anglicans despise that gift and the meagerness of the Protestant name. Let them long again for the rich mystery of medieval culture. As for me I honor the name "Protestant." "Christian" is preferable. But "Lutheran," "Calvinist," "Covenanter," if they separate me from the Reformation in which we all share, is a poor substitute for that red badge of courage.

Agreeable Albert

Maxim for
Moppets

One of the maxims which our Christian culture attempts to teach its young is that agreeableness is a virtue. Boys and girls are taught that cheerful obedience is the way to blessedness and that meekness, deference, lowliness, complaisance will be rewarded both in this life and in the life to come.

Once in a while the persuasiveness of the teacher is such that a child actually becomes what he is taught. There emerges in the world an Agreeable Albert who does what he is asked to do and never demands a pay raise, and who through days devoid of ease applies consistently the Doctrine of the Doormat. When this rare person appears, a little stooped and dazed perhaps but smiling through his tears, his appeal is so strong that men and women weep uncontrollably. When Albert dies, pilgrimages are made to his grave and a mound of flowers witnesses to the fact that though dead, he speaks.

The Power of
Uncle Tom

In the mind of the American people the "good" Negro has always been cast as the Agreeable Albert. This is what some southerners and northerners mean by the "educated nigger"; he is the Negro who bears every indignity with a good-natured smile.

Now there is no question that this Negro is loved. Europeans who look at America across three thousand miles of salt water and who judge us by what happens in Little Rock, sometimes make the mistake of believing that we hate the Negroes *en masse*. Actually, we don't hate Negroes at all as long as they will remain Agreeable Alberts who clean our houses, shine our shoes, smile at us in dining cars, play sweet music, win our Olympics, and *know their place*.

The Meaning of
Place

I had the dubious privilege of spending some of my childhood years in a semifeudal society. I know something about what it means to be cribbed and kenneled and to be not quite accepted. To peek through the palings at the Big House. To long, to envy, to adore, and to despair. I know also that meekness is a way to keep this splendid world orderly. The Agreeable Alberts guarantee that not one silken thread of the Gobelin tapestry is disturbed. The fruit hangs gold-orbed, the gravelled walks sweep by tended and vacant lawns, the water of the palace pond reflects only the proud stateliness of swans.

160

Blessed Are
the Meek

I know also that the meek are blessed. Agreeable Albert
has his reward. When he speaks or sings or laughs or weeps,
the proud world stops to listen. And in Heaven God's throne
is surrounded by his kind, for only Agreeable Albert can
talk with God about the meaning of grace.

Surly Morning

But what I long for now and then is a world in which
all the Agreeable Alberts have been called away and in
which all the exploiters who have fattened on their goodness and their meekness, whose days have been gladdened
by their unassumingness, will confront nothing but surli-
ness. A world in which everyone refuses to be bullied,
cajoled, or used. A world without any give. An iron world,
cold as a filing cabinet and precise as an IBM card. I long
for this world because it would be an honest judgment not
only on the Simon Legrees but on all oily politicians who
have walked to power over the Agreeable Alberts.

And this is the world we are going to have. Sooner or
later the nice people will vanish or harden. The worm will
turn.

A high-school student who has competed against Negroes
for several years said to me the other day, "The Negroes
are much nicer than the whites. They are nicer when they
win and they are nicer when they lose. *I wish we'd give
them a chance.*"

I wish we'd give *ourselves* a chance before the candlestick
is removed and we lose the blessing of our opportunity.

Fantasian Flu

The Fortunes of a
Hypochondriac

The pun in the title is not mine, but I shall take the liberty of using it. I have just risen from a minor illness: a cold complicated by a slight temperature (taken frequently), weakness, and a lack of solidity in reality contact. I am sure I would have thought nothing of it and would probably have ridden out the storm without bed rest and aspirin if I hadn't heard since last summer of the Asian Flu. There were rumors in European ports of ghostly ships riding at anchor in which crew and passengers lay victims of the new plague. As the rumors fattened, the scene became touched with the bizarre. Now they were no longer sick people but bodies deprived of breath and stacked like cordwood.

I am not in any sense belittling the seriousness of the epidemic or the sensible measures which are being taken to cope with it. I am grateful to medical science for everything it does for us, and it does a great deal. One of these days I shall be lining up with my fellow citizens with my arm bared.

But what I do want to say emphatically is that the present epidemic as it is developing in the newspapers is a serious strain on those of us who happen to be hypochondriacs.

Major Sufferers

I do not belong to the Major Pathophobes (those having an abnormal fear of illness). I do not walk around with cotton in my ears. I do not object to talking to people on the phone when they have the sniffles. I do not turn the doorhandle of a public lavatory with a paper towel wrapped around my hand. Nor after a ride on the streetcar do I swab my nasal membranes with an antiseptic. But I am one of the minor sufferers. As soon as the first fat headlines about an epidemic hits the paper, I begin to feel symptoms. And when the telephone begins to report the first cases in the neighborhood, I am an infected, if not quite dead, duck.

Pall Over Christmas

I remember getting a copy of *Borden of Yale* for Christmas when I was still a very young hypochondriac. The story depressed me. It was a Protestant saint's legend, and at fifteen I felt the virtues of Borden of Yale to be not only unattainable but unbelievable. It is nevertheless possible that I could have survived the book if Borden had not died

163

of *cerebro-spinal meningitis*. But that did it. I fled the dark blue cover and the gold imprint like the literal plague. In an irrational way I felt that the writer of the book, and even Borden himself, had conspired to spoil my holiday. For several mornings I felt my forehead, rotated my head briskly to see if my neck was stiffening, and looked for other tell-tale symptoms.

I do not want to bore my readers or fellow sufferers with any detailed account of my growth into hypochondriac maturity. It is with this as with physical symptoms. They interest only the sufferer. But during my long and reasonably healthy years I have lived through in my fancy the symptoms of cancer, Hodgkins disease, cardiac collapse, tuberculosis, total deafness (when my watch had stopped), the various types of desperate dysentery, polio, botulism (after eating some vague sausages), and our old friend meningitis.

Ministry of
Mercy

The latter fear, which was almost my undoing, served in a peculiar way to give me a little saner attitude toward myself. One December night, 1942, in Camp Polk, the Division Chaplain's Office got an urgent call from the Station Hospital. It concerned a man dying of meningitis, and, since I was junior, I was asked to go. I can still recall the groveling fear with which I approached the contagious ward. I was met at the door by a nurse who with good cheer bustled me toward the sickroom. On the way I mumbled thickly about a mask, but she didn't hear me. I stepped warily into the room. I saw my first meningitis sufferer. The man was in a coma and he had the severe rash which I knew was a symptom of his disease. I went through the motion of praying for him, but I was holding my breath for fear of sucking in the infection, and I was screaming in my heart for my own deliverance: "Lord, take care of me, me, me." I learned very little about meningitis that night but I learned something about myself.

There was in me a buffoon of Satan—an abject little mousie with vibrating whiskers and a fiercely terrified heart. Deep within there was a squeak and a scurry from which in my mortal life I should never be delivered.

And No Nonsense

Never the Twain Shall Meet

I have just returned from a conference of Protestant clergymen in which the subject of "mixed" marriage was considered. Both Protestants and Roman Catholics have given the problem serious consideration, particularly since the beginning of World War II when contacts between young people of both persuasions were multiplied. During the discussions a pamphlet prepared by the Roman Church was distributed. It was Monsignor J. D. Conway's *What They Think About Marriage: Catholic and non-Catholic.* From this pamphlet I quote two paragraphs which may help us to a better understanding of ourselves as Protestants. Monsignor Conway is answering a question relative to Roman Catholics' attendance at Protestant worship:

> One basic principle is very clear, and it offers no exception. We can never take *active* part in non-Catholic public worship. The First Commandment of God absolutely forbids it, and Canon 1258

of the Code of Canon Law makes it very clear. Even the Pope could not grant a dispensation from this law. God simply forbids us to worship Him in a false manner. All non-Catholic worship is false because it is not true. The only true worship is that established by Jesus Christ. It is found only in the Church of Christ—the Catholic Church.

God may be pleased with sincere Protestant worship offered to Him by Protestants who are in good faith. He would be offended if Catholics—who know better—were to join with Protestants in offering Him that same false worship. These Catholics would not be sincere or in good faith—unless they were very ignorant.

Thanks to the Monsignor

In a time filled with perplexity we Protestants should be thankful to Monsignor Conway for a firm word about ourselves. Rarely has the Protestant position been sketched with such bold lines. We learn that we have a false faith because the first commandment says that we shall have no other Gods before Yahweh. We are also told that even though we have a false faith which violates the First Commandment at Canon 1258, God is probably pleased with it if we are sincere and are faithful to our flickering lamp. Finally, we are assured that the reason that God accepts our false faith as if it were true is that we don't know any better.

Now on the surface this seems quite logical. We have a

false faith but because we are ignorant, like the savages, the imbeciles, and the very young, divine charity accepts our unacceptable offering.

But the logic is only superficial. What the Roman Church would *like* to say is that Protestant Christians like Mohammedans, head-hunters, and hairy Ainus are outside salvation. Let us not imagine that within the demesne of the hierarchy there sprouts any tender grass of mercy for the erring sheep. How the Roman Church really feels about Protestants was evident in the fizzle of Father Feeney of Boston, who dared to say what every bishop would like to say: Protestants are not within the church; only the church saves; *therefore* Protestants are damned. The same feeling about Protestants burned in the eyes of a Jesuit I once met. He lumped all non-Catholics together: Protestants, Taoists, the gentler Cannibals, and the Great Apes of the Tanga-Outre.

The Roman
Laity

But if this is how the hierarchy feels, why is it that Father Feeney has lost favor and must preach in parks and on street corners in the Holy City of Boston? And why isn't my friend the Jesuit elevated to the red hat? The answer is simple. The Roman Church is not happy about Protestants, but it acts with characteristic prudence. To say to its laity that Protestants who build churches dedicated to Christ, read their Bible, practice baptism and communion according to the Scriptural injunctions, and are not much different in their daily walk from the faithful—to say that these Protestants are lost souls might be most inexpedient. It is much better to term them fools and to hand them over to the tender mercies of God.

Thanks to Father Feeney

Personally, I would rather be called a heretic or pagan than a well-intentioned dolt. I think Father Feeney has paid us Protestants a genuine compliment by refusing to us the cup of salvation. He, at least, makes the lines clear. That does not mean that I favor religious strife. It does not mean that I cannot co-operate with the Roman Church in any endeavor for the public good. Nor that I cannot have and value Roman Catholic friends. What it does mean is that I call a spade a spade. This may help our young people who flirt with the idea of taking Roman instructions to see that the gulf between us is deep and wide. Outside the church there is no salvation, and we can take our pick of churches. But we can't have it both ways.

On Dragging Your Feet

The Hardness
of God

For a decade and a half I have been an eager reader of C. S. Lewis, but nothing in his books has struck me with quite the force of a paragraph in his autobiographical *Surprised by Joy*. He is describing his conversion:

You must picture me alone in that room in Magdalen, night after night, feeling, whenever my mind lifted even for a second from my work, the steady unrelenting approach of him whom I so earnestly desired not to meet. That which I greatly feared had at last come upon me. In the Trinity Term of 1929 I gave in, and admitted that God was God, and knelt and prayed: perhaps that night, the most dejected and reluctant convert in all England. I did not then see what is now the most shining and obvious thing: the Divine humility which will accept a convert even on such terms. The Prodigal Son at least walked home on his own feet. But who can duly adore that Love which will open the high gates to a prodigal who is brought in kicking, struggling, resentful, and darting his eyes in every direc-

tion for a chance to escape? . . . The hardness of God is
kinder than the softness of men, and His compulsion is our
liberation.

Divine
Compulsion

It is just as well to begin by setting the record straight.
I may not have been so reluctant a convert as Mr. Lewis.
My process of justification was, as I recall it, neither so
long nor so laborious as his. But, alas, my sanctification has
proceeded in much the manner that he describes. I have
been all my life a "kicking, struggling, dejected, and reluctant" Christian.

I have just completed the annual routine of getting my
storm windows up. This is ahead of schedule since we
are not yet in the Advent season, and the blizzard I en-
countered on the day I started the task lacked its mid-
season fury. But whatever joy I may have felt in improving
on my schedule was muddied by the thought to which
I was driven by contemplating dirty panes, crumbling putty,
and peeling paint.

I saw all my life reflected in the glass before me. It seemed
to me that I approach every task, even the most exalted,
with the same tentativeness and distaste which I felt in the
presence of these windows. I get it done. Once the pres-
sures begin to nudge and prod me, I do the job. The gas
bill climbs, our guests ask for shawls and sweaters, the
children have sniffles, the blinds rattle. Then I lay a heavy
hand on my own collar and the windows get up.

Duty Whispers
Low

I am asked for a talk. Lacking both the imagination to foresee what I am doing or the courage to act upon my conviction, I agree to do what I am asked. Then the torture begins. First, I get comfort in the thought that I need not do this dreaded Thing today or tomorrow. There is still some time left. Like a capital prisoner awaiting the tumbril which is to take him to the gallows, I count the hours and the minutes before the Thing. I awaken in the morning with the question: Is It today? If not, I have a little flurry of happiness. But the Thing approaches and I am finally driven to prepare myself. This is always done the day before, the night before, or the morning of the Thing. Before my departure for the assignment, I am in a lather of nervous excitability. I cut myself while shaving, get the bath water too hot, fall into a heavy neurotic sleep which sends me back into consciousness unfocussed and imbecilic, and inevitably misplace my car keys. I arrive at my destination tense, bug-eyed, and with a conviction that what I have to say is trite or confused or just dull.

The Youth
Replies

I envy, oh, I envy, the preacher who loves to preach, the writer who loves to write, the houseowner who loves to get into something comfy and just putter around. I would like to bequeath them my tasks. They seem so competent, so joyously engaged, so easily rewarded. They spread an aura of happiness about them; nurses bringing the morning bath, brisk masseurs, cooks basting their roasts with delight, flower girls offering violets and lyrics by the town fountain. Ah, happy breed, what secret of inward tranquility is yours?

God's Surly Man

But Lewis is right. God's mercy is so great that even when we drag our feet He compels us to do what we are called to do. This is our salvation. Even those who sigh and grumble, and stew and fret, even God's surly men, as long as they are God's, are allowed to enter the land of peace. Shall we lift up our hoarse and reluctant voices?

The Torch of Smoky Pine

The Palace of
Memory

The phrase is Augustine's. The great church father was impressed by our ability to retain within the narrow compass of our skulls the vastness and complexity of the known world. But what we know is past. The known stretches out behind us like the trail left by a ship. About the future we know little or nothing. The bow of the ship is shrouded in fog. "Our knowledge," said George Santayana, "is like a torch of smoky pine which lights the pathway but one step ahead, across the void of mystery and dread."

I have been walking this past week through the palace of memory. Room 1929 claimed my attention. A memorable year, it began in splendor. A soaring stock market and the promise of universal chicken dinners and the new Ford with stick shift was like the heady invitation of that year's hit song, "Come tip-toe through the tulips with me." America dressed in white flannels, a blue coat, and pointed black and white shoes was off for a romp in the tulips.

There is no need to rehearse the symptoms of financial

drunkenness from 1929; sober people were turned into amiable touts. They borrowed, they speculated, they bought stock on the margin, they spent with gay abandon. I remember considering seriously the withdrawing of 45 dollars from my savings account and buying ¼ of a lot in the vicinity of Milton Dam, Ohio. The lot was probably submerged under the dam waters, but in 1929 even marsh bottom glittered with promise. In any event, I thought better of it and invested my money in a secondhand trumpet, to the sorrow of our neighbors, who would rather have had me a land baron in Milton Dam than a struggling cornetist next door. But when the crash came Art triumphed over Finance and I was left unscathed.

Most Disastrous Day

I was one of the few lucky ones. There were not many in 1929. On October 23 Wall Street was shaken by the beginnings of a panic. The number of stock transfers skyrocketed, the market began to slip tether and by the end of the day losses totalled 4 million on the New York Exchange. I am not competent to make a financial analysis of the disaster, but I have read with great interest the comments which filled the papers after the event. They sound like nothing so much as the sage observations of doctors gathered around the sick bed of a great man. British financial wizards, French specialists, American geniuses, Italian tycoons all stroked their beards and proclaimed the patient ill but rallying. The decline was attributed to "overproduction," "underconsumption," "panic among inexperienced stockholders," a useful "corrective action," a "stabilizing influence," and a hundred other things; but on one point there seems to have been near unanimity: there would be improvement, gradually but sure. The patient would not die. He was sick, how sick no one could say for certain, but this was not sickness unto death. Oh, no! This was a beneficial purge, a happy hemorrhage, a symptom of turbulent humors, but nothing to be alarmed about. The market would recover. Of course it would. It had before. Remember how it was in 1928 when everyone predicted, etc., etc.? One of the doctors proclaimed his faith in the patient by pouring his immense personal resources into a stock buying project. And wonder of wonders, the patient rallied. The thready pulse became full and regular. Color returned to the pale face. Breathing seemed less labored. The invalid fluttered his eyelids and a few hours later asked for soup. "Soup, soup!" rang the word through the corridors, "the patient wants soup!"

Thus on the 25th, the 26th, the 27th, the 28th. The convalescent was surrounded by sirupy and soothing voices, telling him how well he looked, how well he had eaten his soup, how soon he would be back at his job with a springy step and bounce in the blood.

Then came the 29th of October, 1929. Up to this time there seems to have been only one Cassandra prophesying doom. This was a man named Roger Babson. Mr. Babson said curtly, "We have not reached bottom." On October 29, Mr. Babson was proved correct. The day was a rout, a wild debacle of selling in which 16,400,000 shares changed hands. The losses were titanic. On the New York Exchange alone the losses mounted to 10 billion dollars, which in 1929 must have seemed the end of the world. Wrote the New York *Tribune*, "This is the most disastrous day in Wall

Street's history." It was to prove a most disastrous day in the history of the nation. Ahead stretched the murky years of bread lines, apple stands, and WPA shovels.

Hindsight

All this can now be seen with a certain clarity. This is how it was and weren't people dopes not to understand what was happening? But we are all dopes and the bow is shrouded in mist. How much do we know today of what tomorrow brings? It is well to remember this lest in castigating the past we have merely ridiculed ourselves.

Angels Without Wings

The Hollow
Thud

I heard a sermon on angels the other day. The man who preached it wanted to be quite sure that everybody understood that he did not believe in the "three story" universe: a heaven in which God sat on a gold chair surrounded by an angelic host; a flat earth; and a basement furnace room. He did not believe in angels with bodies and wings. He did not say, but I suppose he also meant, that he did not believe in angels with voices. He claimed to believe in angels but what he conjured up was something unwinging and unsinging—a fuzzy emanation. And he gave us the old argument that since God is a Spirit he should not be thought as being above us. He is everywhere. The image which suggested itself was that of a ubiquitous and benevolent gas.

For many years now sober-minded people have been at work trying to make the message of the Bible more rational. They feel that the Bible has a great truth to communicate but that the world view of the Bible and the language in which it is expressed stand in the way of its acceptance by the scientifically trained. "How," say these people, "can you make a skeptic believe in a God with a long white beard? Who sits on a chair above the clouds? Who makes man out of mud? Who eats a roast with Abraham? How can you make a perceptive modern person believe that disease is caused by demons, that bread and fish can be multiplied, that a man can walk on water? What we have to do, say these well-intentioned people, is to peel away this crude outer layer and get at the truth hidden within. We have to develop a Christian faith which is palatable for modern man."

Simile of an Onion

But the peeling of Biblical truth is not like removing the rind of an orange; it is like going to work on an onion. What is the essential onion? We may say that the essential orange is what is found under the peeling. But the essence of an onion is peeling, layer upon layer of it. The essence of the Bible is "crude anthropomorphism." There is not a single Biblical truth which does not personify God. While it is true that we are made in his image and not he in ours, the very idea of imaging forth suggests that the God of the Bible is not "wholly other" but radically personal. We may be able to eliminate the white beard but not much more. Whatever his omnipresence means, it is more like a visitation than the constancy of a meteorological factor. And if God's fatherhood has any significance it must lie not so much in his capacity to cause as in his desire to create and in his terrifying love of the created.

179

Naivete and Maturity

The Biblical world is very much like medieval painting. There was a time in my schooling when medieval painters were spoken of with condescension because they had not "solved" the problem of perspective. They put human figures in the distance which were as high as mountains. They had no way of showing the convergence of parallel lines in recession. In other words, they painted like children. Then came the Renaissance and people like Da Vinci and Rembrandt made things look the way they "really" are.

I need hardly say that this judgment of medieval art is now outmoded. We no longer smile loftily when we see a medieval painting in which a room doesn't look like a room. In a strange way we let the world of medieval art captivate us and determine its own criteria. The same may be said of Dante. We do not regard Dante with smugness because he puts Hell in the bowels of our planet. We do not ask poets to submit their infernal blueprints to a scientific zoning board. Nor do we suggest that Dante would be improved if we rewrote his poem so as to conform with our science.

What we are becoming aware of, at least in some circles, is that poets and painters come closer to the truth of things than we do with all our scientific apparatus. Perhaps one reason that Dante's Hell is more Hellish than Milton's— more awesome, more terrifying, more somberly beautiful— is that Dante was less worried than Milton about astronomical findings. Milton uses the old astronomy, but he is aware of the new, perhaps too much so.

The effort to give us a Christianity without the incarnation, without miracles, without the Resurrection and Ascension, without angels and demons is undoubtedly the work of sincere, gifted, and humble men. They want to give us a Scriptural theorem which will be unembarrassed by modern science. I predict their failure. What we shall get will not be Christianity at all, but a de-horned and de-winged homunculus which will leave us where we are, unterrified and unconsoled.